An Alban
Institute
Publication

POWER &
CHANGE

IN PARISH
MINISTRY

*Reflections on the
Cure of Souls*

MICHAEL JINKINS

DEBORAH BRADSHAW JINKINS

As clergy, you are called to be curate ("a caretaker of souls"), charged both to heal and lead your congregation as its members seek wholeness. It is this role, perhaps more than any other, that plunges you into the complex issues of authority, power, and change in your ministerial leadership. How do you heal yet still lead and guide? How well do you use the power that comes with this role to effect change? Can you alone, in fact, effect change? Join Michael Jinkins (D. Min., Ph.D., active Presbyterian pastor) and Deborah Jinkins (M.A. Ed. Admin., educational consultant) as they guide you through an examination of this most crucial of your roles. Your will draw on theological, sociological, educational, and managerial viewpoints (some of them never before applied to congregations) to examine your ministry. You will learn from others' experiences and use a set of self-assessment instruments to analyze your ministry and integrate your findings.

*An Alban
Institute
Publication*

POWER &
CHANGE
IN PARISH
MINISTRY

Reflections on the Cure of Souls

MICHAEL JINKINS
DEBORAH BRADSHAW JINKINS

References on pages 30 and 31 of Chapter II to John Kenneth Galbraith's work are from *The Anatomy of Power* by John Kenneth Galbraith. Copyright © 1983 by John Kenneth Galbraith. Reprinted by permission of Houghton Mifflin Co..

The Publications Program of The Alban Institute is assisted by a grant from Trinity Church, New York City.

Library of Congress Catalog Card #90-86199
ISBN 1-56699-042-4

For our friends
in
Saint Stephen's Presbyterian Church, Irving, Texas
First Presbyterian Church, Itasca, Texas
The Beechgrove Church, Aberdeen, Scotland
and
Brenham Presbyterian Church, Brenham, Texas
beside whom we have served
and with whom we have shared this life and ministry.

CONTENTS

The best way to begin this book is to explain that we began it all wrong. Our first idea was to begin by producing a paper on the interrelated subjects of power and change, looking into the way in which insights from the disciplines of sociology, psychology, and educational theory might inform parish ministry. We planned to begin by delving into the secondary sources on the subject of power and change, then to move on to the peculiarities of the church as a social grouping. Fortunately, this original plan did not get off the ground. Fortunately, that is, because to have begun this book from the entry point of sociology, psychology, and educational theory would have caused us to set off on rather an inappropriate road. The road we *have* chosen to take values the insights we derived from these disciplines, but it places these insights within a different frame, a practical theological frame.

The catalyst that caused us to abandon the original design for this book was contained in a letter from Celia Hahn last year. We had written Celia with the idea for a book on power and change in the congregation. She handed the letter along to Loren Mead. He responded by saying that his concern with our plan was that it seemed to offer only a "two-dimensional" treatment of a "three-dimensional issue." "That is," he continued, "this feels psychological and sociological, but this is on 'religious authority.'" He recommended that we do the psychological and sociological work, but that we also explore more fully the "religious" dimension. He summed up our original plan by saying: "I think this prospectus misses the important, but messy, inchoate issues of power and change in things like sacraments, the mystical, the relation of pastor to church member, the dimension of God's power in spoken Word." To Loren and Celia we owe the enormous debt of providing us the impetus to turn around and face the other way in exploring this tangled and vital issue of congregational power and change.

The result of this *metanoia* has been, first, a delay in producing this book as we reflected more seriously on the personal, spiritual dimensions of power and change in the parish. This delay has been aggravated by the research Michael was doing, until recently, in pursuance of his Ph.D. in Systematic Theology at King's College, the University of Aberdeen, Scotland, and Deborah's crowded schedule as a member of the faculty of the American School in Aberdeen and as an educational consultant. Second, and more positively, this change of mind has resulted in a radical shift in the entire study we hoped to produce. What lies before you is a very personal account of our own pilgrimage, a pilgrimage we have endeavored to report with honesty and vigor, a journey that has been informed by our forays into sociology, psychology, and educational theory, but which remains thoroughly a movement of faith.

How to Use This Resource

It was our intention to provide a book that could (above all else) be used in the actual life of a parish. However, it was also our intention, from the beginning, to provide a book that provides a wealth of observations, research, and reflection in a readable format.

In order to achieve both of these goals, we put together a book that contains a text, looking into the dynamics of power and change in the pastor-parish relationship. And, so that this book will prove especially practical, we have included an appendix of instruments to use in the pastor's personal reflection, several tools that s/he can utilize in his or her own analysis of him/herself and the congregation. We have designed the book in such a way so as to be read at a variety of levels, tapping the cognitive and rational aspects of the pastor's reflections as well as the intuitive, emotive, and affectional. The instruments in the appendix are designed to assist the pastor in looking and listening to his or her own pastor-parish relationship. And again, they are designed to assist the pastor in listening and looking in a way that taps cognitive, rational, intuitive, and emotional and affectional aspects of the personality.

We have begun in several places to develop some theological reflections that we hope the pastor will continue to work through. In many ways, the emergence of these reflections (as basic as they obviously are) was the most exciting area developed in the book, though perhaps the most "messy." The comments we have provided in this context will, we hope, serve as a springboard in the reader's own theological reflections on parish ministry.

Acknowledgments

We particularly want to express our appreciation to Celia Hahn and Loren Mead, without whose support and encouragement this book would not have been possible. We want to thank Dr. Louis Adams, Director of the Pastoral Counseling Center at Brite Divinity School, Texas Christian University, Ft. Worth, Texas, for the valuable insights he contributed to our work and for the additional observations he provided from his own experience and research. We also want to thank Mrs. Janie Coffin Baker of Itasca, Texas, for agreeing to read the entire manuscript and to lend her observations from the perspective of an informed and active layperson.

We shall acknowledge specifically the sources of research and other observations that enriched this study in the footnotes throughout the book. But a special word of thanks goes to the many anonymous pastors and laypersons whose experiences form the observational basis of our study and, in a fictionalized form, are chronicled here.

Finally, we dedicate this book to our friends, the parishioners beside whom we have served over the years at St. Stephen's Presbyterian Church, Irving, Texas; First Presbyterian Church, Itasca, Texas; The Beechgrove Church (Church of Scotland) Aberdeen, Scotland; and Brenham Presbyterian Church, Brenham, Texas.

Michael and Deborah Jinkins
Brenham, Texas
Feastday of St. Bernard of Clairvaux, 1990

The Title Page Says It All

The title page pretty much says it all. This is a pastor's tool, a reflective guidebook to assist clergy in understanding the dynamics of power and change in the parish setting as they go about the extraordinarily complex ministry thar we are describing as "the cure of souls."

We shall consider actual parish situations, drawn from real life,[1] reflecting on each of them from a variety of perspectives in order to learn how we may best serve as pastoral ministers in this complex web of parochial power and change. Our method will be to invite the reader to assume *the active posture of reflection*. The narratives and reflection sections are designed to call forth the reader's critical and intuitive skills.

We hope our own analyses—in light of various sociological, educational, managerial, *and* theological viewpoints—will prove useful to the reader. But, even more, we hope the reader will be spurred on to test our analyses, to go beyond the boundaries of our views, and then to integrate the analytical model into his or her own pastoral ministry.

A "Cure of Souls"

We have a hero, the most heroic sort of hero, the common garden variety of hero: the curate. We have read about curates toiling quietly in the village churches in fourteenth-century England, providing spiritual comfort to comfortless victims of the plague, extending hospitality to pilgrims, administering the sacraments in cold and damp sanctuaries, carving out their own special place in the life of the village. We have watched them through the eyes of Anthony Trollope in nineteenth-century Victorian society, often on the fringe of the social crowd or resigned to an uncelebrated corner, looking curiously amusing, but upheld with a remarkable and almost unearthly dignity.

The curates (*in name*) whom we have known personally during those years in which we lived in Britain were usually honorary curates, most often university dons who maintained a functional connection with a parish by preaching occasionally. But there were many clergy who performed tirelessly the work of curate who were called virtually everything from minister to pastor to rector or vicar.

What these genuine curates all have in common is the particular locus of their pastoral ministry. They are not primarily denominational officials, representatives of the larger or wider church, or clerical specialists. They are grandly "generalists" whose ministry is focused among a particular local congregation. Their concern is for the cure of souls, especially those souls that have been entrusted to their pastoral care. We have come to believe that this particular hero, the curate, makes a superb role model for our work of parish ministry, especially if we can understand the way s/he is meant to function.

The word "curate" that we are so loosely tossing about derives from the responsibility of having a "cure of souls." But the word "cure," perhaps surprisingly, does not mean primarily "to make well" or "to restore to health." Although we all recognize pastoral ministry, in a real sense, to involve a "healing" dimension, a concern to assist parishioners to achieve a sense of wholeness, the primary meaning of this "cure" refers to the exercise of administrative power. The term "cure" from which the word "curate" derives its meaning has a Latin and French background and means "to have charge over."

The Oxford Dictionary defines the curate as follows:

"One entrusted with the cure of souls; a spiritual pastor."

Generally the word may apply to "any ecclesiastic (including a bishop, etc.) who has the spiritual charge of a body of laymen." But more precisely the word refers to:

"A clergyman who has the spiritual charge of a parish...;
a parson of a parish."

The earliest source the dictionary notes for the word is from the fourteenth century, where the curate is described as one having "cure and souerante ouer othir men forto teche and reule hem."[2]

The word curate is not a particularly familiar one to most of us today, but the etymology of this word can serve us as a sort of historical analogy pointing to the practical reality in our life of the local congregation. In pastoral ministry the exercise of power and authority is part and parcel of our caring and healing ministry. The two cannot be separated into clearly discrete spheres. The curate has always been concerned with the *healing* cure of souls, but he or she cannot divorce this *healing* cure from the *ruling* cure. In order for us to be successful and effective in our care giving, we must understand how to deal with power and change in a manner appropriate to our calling.

"Power," Roy Oswald wrote several years ago, "is the ability to get what you want."[3] If it is the purpose of the pastoral minister, the "curate," to effect the healing cure of his or her people, then s/he must also take seriously the practical dynamics of power. To do otherwise is to abandon one's vocational responsibility. *This is why this book has been written, to help pastors come to terms with the entire spectrum of their "cure of souls."*

The dynamics of power, however, cannot be understood unless we also consider the dynamics of change. A pastor is a human being, a growing, developing creature, a person who (it is hoped!) is being drawn into Christlikeness. A congregation is a body of persons, growing, developing, sharing in certain creaturely characteristics but individually unique in a multitude of ways. Change is a part of the game from the word go. And if this is not understood, then nothing else can be.

The cure of souls requires that the pastor understand his or her role both as representative of the corporate body in its persistence and as change agent. On the one hand, the pastor represents a sense of continuity on behalf of the congregation, while, on the other hand, s/he acts as a catalyst upon the congregation to encourage healthful change. Should the pastor represent too fully the congregation's corporate persistence, stagnation will occur. But if the pastor becomes merely an irritant, the congregation will disown him or her.

The dynamics of power and change interrelate in a number of other ways, as we shall observe. But at the heart of the "cure of souls" is the professional clergy's dual relationship to power and change.

Christ As Curate over All Souls

Finally, as we reflect on the cure of souls from a theological perspective, we find the essential clue to our vocation in Christ's own cure of souls. In fact, it would be appropriate to describe Christ as the eternal Curate who holds the cure over all souls, in whom we find our curacy defined, realized, and fulfilled, and by whom we are enabled to carry out the ministry of cure. In the same way that Christ is the one true Liturgist (*Leitourgos*), he is the one true Curate in whose pastoral ministry we participate by the power of the Holy Spirit and in light of whose curacy we serve.[4] Having said this, we have of course described the perimeters of our ministry of cure as being that which conforms to Christ. This very basic theological reflection will serve us as we attempt to understand the source of our spiritual authenticity (Chapter 1), the proper exercise of pastoral authority (Chapter 2), and the development of change in the parish (Chapter 3).

These three general areas of concern provide us with a sort of conceptual framework upon which we can hang our observations. And so it is to the first of these general concerns we shall now turn our attention as we attempt to understand the relationship between power and spiritual authenticity in the parish.

NOTES

1. All pastor-parish anecdotes, unless otherwise indicated, have been fictionalized to protect the identity of those involved.
2. *The Compact Edition of the Oxford English Dictionary* (Oxford: Oxford University Press, 1971), 1259.
3. Roy M. Oswald, *Power Analysis of a Congregation* (Washington, DC: The Alban Institute, 1981, reprinted 1988), 3.
4. This parallel is suggested generally in James B. Torrance, "The Place of Jesus Christ in Worship," *Theological Foundations for Ministry*, Ray S. Anderson, editor (Edinburgh/Grand Rapids: T.&T. Clark/Wm. Eerdmans, 1979), 348n.

CHAPTER I

Power and Authenticity

"We do heartily invite, call and entreat you to undertake the office of a
pastor among us and the charge of our souls."

—The ancient form of congregational
call in the Scottish Kirk

"Lest you be overwhelmed with the greatness of your task,
remember no church is given to any man without the Savior of the
church and of him. After all it is Christ's church, and the Bishop of its
minister. You are but his curate."

—P.T. Forsyth

A Faerie Tale

Once upon a time
          long, long ago
                    in a land, far, far away...

The Story of the Seventh Thane

The Seventh Thane of Rothiemurchus drank deeply the dregs of failure,
his own failure and a failure his people also shared, for he had been
given a marvelous gift and he had abused and lost it. Almost in a moment, in the twinkling of an eye, he had lost the myterious gift handed
down from generation to generation in the family of lairds of
Rothiemurchus. And with the loss of the mysterious gift, he had nearly
lost his fiefdom. For a moment his future and theirs had teetered on a
precipice. A wisp of down could have sent them all tumbling to their
separate fates.

This had begun to happen even before the auld brig at Coylum-
bridge was built, when River Bruie was forded just below the mound of
grey stone, long before the Queen's forest was hunted out. But all these
things came as blessings and curses upon the heels of the thane's folly
(as it was called ever after).

It began as all true stories begin, "once upon a time," when the
thane was a young man and eager to learn the ways of the ruler. He was
given the gift to speak a word, a secret word in a secret voice. The word
was given him by the Black Sorcerer of Urquhart when the young man
became the seventh thane after his father the old thane's death. The voice
came from somewhere deeply hidden. Some said from the gods. Some
said from deep inside the thane himself. Some said the voice processed
from the people or from the life that was created between the thane and
his people. No one knows for certain. And perhaps that is not important,
but what is important is that the secret word the thane spoke in his secret
voice healed those who heard its sound. The voice sounded like roaring
waters crashing down on granite slabs. But it was not a frightening voice,
though ever so loud. Rather it was the voice of pure love, proceeding

from someplace deep and still and quiet, like a hidden stream that sur-
faces suddenly in a rushing cataract, spilling mercy on all that stand
beneath its flow.

And thus he ruled. As his father the old thane had ruled, so ruled
he. Or thus he was meant to rule. After the old thane died on the field of
battle near Loch Gamhna, the young thane took his place on the sacred
chair and heard the oath of fealty from his people and swore his oath of
fealty to his people, as is the custom in Rothiemurchus. And then and
there the new thane received the power to speak the healing word.

During the early days of his reign the young thane did well. The
people did not know what to expect from him. But they had no reason to
expect ill. They smiled at him when he appeared at the village merchat
cross. They sang to him the doxology of kings when he appeared at the
sacred ring. And they wept for joy when he spoke his word and healed
the paralytic child at Creag Follais, after the pilgrimage to Baileguish
when the sacred hags held court beneath the stone table.

All went very well in these very early days.

An Arrival of Strangers

They say that it was about this time that two strangers came into the
fiefdom. Fenner, the strong man of Dunnottar, reputed to be the wisest
and darkest adviser of princes in all the North, arrived when the winter
winds had just begun to gust. He moved into the castle and took to ad-
vising the thane from the moment he arrived. About this same time came
Egberth the Sauchebum poet, who sang ballads and brave songs at courts
throughout the land. He was wise also, but with another wisdom as
everyone soon found out.

Fenner's wisdom was the deep wisdom of the worldly wise. He
understood the magic of grasping and holding. And he taught his subtle
laws to the thane. He balanced the books of the heart with cruel gravity,
teaching the young thane to value retribution and self-preservation. His
darkness he wrapped about himself like a regal robe. And he strode the
parapets of the thane's tower house like a gathering storm.

The poet sang the songs of the wounded gods, the gods who lay
themselves low for the sake of love. He sang of the kings who served for
the sake of the wounded gods. He sang of the people who would die
rather than wound one another. He sang melodious music that needed

voices joined to his. He brought everyone into the songs. And somehow, in the singing, everyone felt at-oned.

All through the winter the thane learned the counsel of Fenner and listened to the music of the poet. The courtiers closest to the seventh thane knew the thane was uneasy. The wisdom of Fenner's magic did not stand well in company with the music of the poet. But the thane listened to both all through the chilled days and nights until spring warmed and the snows melted. Then he set himself to the task of practicing the wisdom he preferred.

Fenner's Dark Magic

Fenner taught the thane how he might manipulate people to the ends he desired, how he might increase his power, how he could keep the things he held and how he could survive every struggle. He showed the thane how to play at power, how to divide to conquer, how to use and grasp and possess.

The magic of Fenner had its own dark charm, and the thane liked the ends it brought him, though sometimes he was disgusted with its means. The thane's war, in early May, with the king of Balavil was one such mean that was unfortunate, though the thane's ruthless victory guaranteed his own security and expanded his territory by untold hides.

Then there were the alterations he made to his castle fortification the coming summer. The taxes he levied became an hardship to the poor, but the castle had to be strengthened if he were to enter the great league of thanes. Appearance of power, Fenner told him many times, was almost as importance as power's acquisition.

And so the fame of the seventh thane grew. He had new robes sewn, with linings of fur and brocade of silver. His horses were the fastest. His building projects were the grandest. This was when the auld brig was built, and the mills that once lined the river. And about this time the thane's extravagant hunting parties nearly emptied the wood of wild creatures.

Something else had begun to happen, though at first few noticed. The thane sent the Sauchieburn poet, Egbert, away from his court sometime before summer came, before his attack upon neighboring Balavil. Some said there had been a terrible row and the thane had threatened to have the poet's head. Others said only that the thane had grown weary of his loathsome lyrics, droning always on about courage and love, and that he knew few ballads beyond the conventional songs of old.

But I believe the poet was sent away because of something that had happened to the thane himself. About this same time, the thane began to lose his voice. Not the voice with which he spoke at court or cried in battle, but his sacred voice, the voice that spoke the word of healing among his people. Something happened within the king himself, and somehow between himself and the people with whom he had sworn his oath. And no longer was heard the word's strange sound that had once, not so long before, caused the paralytic to dance.

The Prophesy of Ilthon

Before the next winter came, Ilthon the Sorcerer of the Great Glenn came down from his season among the high craigs of the Cairngorms, where he dwelt alone in the shadow of Carn a'Mhaim not far from the Devil's Point. It had been a full year since last he laid eyes on the thane. And when he saw the thane draped in his rich robes of state, followed closely by Fenner, the sorcerer wailed and tore his cloak and threw dust into the air and uttered holy and frightening oaths. The sorcerer pointed his finger at the thane and said he had taken evil counsel. He prophesied there and then, even without having been in our fiefdom during those eventful months, that the king no longer possessed his sacred voice, and that, unless something happened to change the thane, he would also lose his fiefdom, for already he had lost his people's love. He no longer held that which was most precious, the power of the healing gift, for he had given himself over to the seduction of the magic of grasp and hold. And then Ilthon rolled his eyes back into his head and sang in his curious dialect,

> Frae beginnin' auld, tae nae, ye kin,
> thy gift is e'er tak'n agin,
> 'chAru thy feif, 'charu ye name,
> 'chAru thy self, 'charu ye same.

The song he sang meant that from time's origin till that moment everyone knew the gift that was given by a people, their loving acceptance of their thane, could be lost as easily as it could be given. To lead his people, he must be true to the people, to his name, to himself, and to his mission. Because he had been untrue and had ruled by means that were unworthy of a thane, he stood in peril of losing all he had been given. Already the losses had begun.

The thane's face went red with rage; his hand reached for the sword hanging at his side. Swiftly, in a single motion, he pulled it from its jeweled scabbard and wielded it above his head in an arch. The crowd drew in its breath and waited, sure that Ilthon's head would tumble into the dust at his feet. But, then, just as quickly the thane went pale for he knew the words of Ilthon were right and honest. In a flash, the thane saw himself reflected in the sorcerer's eyes. The thane knew that he had been untrue to his people and his name, to himself and to the healing mission to which he was commissioned when he assumed his rule.

The thane turned and looked hard into the faces of his people. And as he did, grace and judgment met him in every eye. He dropped the sword onto the ground and slowly sank to his knees, bowing his head over till it touched the ground. The sorcerer spoke truly as the mouthpiece of this silent answering sorrow.

Fenner bent down to whisper to the thane. "Get up, your majesty," he whispered. "Get up. Send this sorcerer to his grave. Forget his spiteful words. Get up. Do not let the people see thee in shame. Get up." But as the thane remained on the ground, tears streaming down his face, Fenner spoke more harshly, in a manner not at all fitting, "Get up, you fool! Can't you see that you are undoing all we have done! Get up or we are finished." The thane remained where he was for a moment longer. Then slowly he pulled himself up. He picked up his sword. Sheathed it. And turning on his heels, he walked slowly back into his castle.

The Return of the Thane

Sometime during the days when the thane was in the castle, a rumor began to circulate that Fenner had been spied late one night stealing away toward the south. At the end of a fortnight the thane came to the merchat cross at the heart of the village and called out to the people to hear him. "I stand before you myself, for I have again come to myself, and I wish you to have me again as your thane. I cannot demand this honour. This is the gift that must be given, by the gods, but also by you.

I hope you will trust me again as once you trusted me. And I hope that
the time will come again when I may heal you, for you have healed me."

The story is told, and I have no reason to doubt it, that the thane,
who was still quite young when all of this happened, lived and ruled and
healed his people until his brown beard had gone grey. It is said that his
sacred voice was restored. And some say that Egberth the poet of
Sauchieburn was sent for and that he came and sang his wisdom until at
last the thane made him the court musician and bade him stay forever.
And never again did Fenner's magic of grasp and hold claim the heart of
the thane, for his people had healed him of its deadly charm.

Not a Faerie Tale

Beginnings

Once upon a time, long ago (long enough ago that finally I can tell the
story), I failed very badly at the one thing I most wanted to do well. It
happened the year after graduating from college. Deborah and I had just
become engaged. She still needed a year to finish her course of study, so
I took a job managing a furniture store in the central Texas town where
our college was located. As it happened, one of my professors recommended me to the search committee of a small rural congregation. I met
the committee, and shortly afterwards they called me as their pastor, with
the understanding that I would serve only for a year, after which time I
would be moving away to study at the seminary.

I was, at that time, a Southern Baptist minister, and as is often the
custom in that tradition, I had been licensed to preach by my "home"
church, the church of my youth. It was not unusual to find young men
like myself, not yet seminary trained, pastoring in small rural churches.

That year was a busy one. Deborah and I were married in Septem-
ber. She finished her senior year and did her student teaching. My work
at the furniture store kept me busy six days a week. Sundays I preached
two services, and Wednesday nights we held prayer meetings. The
church's being forty miles from the town in which we lived made it difficult but not unbearable. From time to time it was necessary for me to
spend a weekend in Dallas for the "markets" where furniture for the store
was purchased. Usually I arranged to preach the Sunday morning service

and made the three-hour drive to Dallas after the service, cancelling the evening service. In that only a very few people showed up on Sunday evenings, I did not perceive this as a problem and neither did the Church—at first.

A Waning of Enthusiasm

In time, the hours and the stresses of "real" life began to take something of a toll on my health. I found myself growing listless and disinterested in my work, both at the furniture store and at the church. My sermons made little allowance for my hearers. I think at first they probably did. But as my enthusiasm and energy waned, I worked less at making the sermons connect. I remember that I was conscious of some distance between myself and the congregation. I had become somewhat enthralled with the sophisticated intellectual world that seemed to await me at seminary, and it showed. Distance grew between myself and my congregation. Not all at once, but inexorably, I distanced myself from them as though I did not share their way of seeing things. They no doubt sensed that I did not see myself "as one of them." Thus we emerged, after the early trial months of our time together, without that bonding that is essential in all lasting, significant relationships.

Within myself (I now know) I was struggling with a change of orientation in my faith. The pain implicit in this struggle was inevitably increased by my own lack of maturity. I could not have known then where this struggle would lead. I could not then have anticipated that I would leave the denominational affiliation of my family, my wife's family, and our closest friends for another faith tradition. But even then, I was becoming aware that I was dissatisfied with the understanding of the "ordinances" of Baptism and the Lord's Supper which I had received in the Baptist tradition.

One of my first disagreements with the deacons of the church was over the Lord's Supper. They observed it only twice a year, a custom that I did not change, but which I protested. They particularly objected to my notion of observing the ordinance on a Sunday morning in order to make it open to more people, especially to the visitors who would be in the community for a high school reunion scheduled for that day. Their concern was that the ordinance should be fenced in and protected from abuse. This they sought to do by restricting attendance at the Supper only to those of their own congregation, those who shared their understanding of the Christian faith. I frankly did not agree with this view. But even more important, I did not respect this view. And this they quickly sensed.

On another occasion a young woman I knew well was denied membership in a nearby Baptist church because she had been baptized in another denomination. She had to undergo a "Baptist baptism" in order to be accepted by that local congregation. I preached a sermon the next week against this practice. The distance grew between myself and the congregation.

"I Just Don't Think You Love Us"

Looking back over a gulf of several years, it seems now that the distance was not so wide between the congregation and myself that the relationship could not have survived. Probably we could have rocked along to the end of my year with them had not one particular incident occurred.

One Tuesday morning, I think it was about seven o'clock, I received a phone call from the wife of one of the deacons. I knew the family well and had stayed often in their home. Their daughter wanted to be married, and they wanted me to do the wedding. "That is great," I said. "When?"

Next Sunday, they said.

I was mildly shocked at the suddenness. And, to be honest, I was more than mildly frightened. I had never performed a wedding before. I had only been to three or four. I had been told by my professors that it is an absolute must for those who take seriously their ministry to do premarital counseling. And, though I haven't the faintest idea what I would have told the couple at that time, I did take seriously my ministry. I told them that I thought I should see them sometime during the week, before Sunday, at the very least to organize the ceremony and to meet the groom. They agreed to come to see me on Saturday.

Friday night they called to say they couldn't make it down to see me. They were simply too busy. They asked if I could drive up to see them. Unfortunately, I explained, I worked all day on Saturday and could not make it. I remember now that they seemed very anxious about my wanting to talk to them, though then I couldn't perceive why. I said that it was really important for a couple to at least talk with their minister before a wedding, otherwise a minister became little more than a reli-

gious functionary, uncritically placing the Church's blessing on whatever comes along. Finally, the couple said that they simply could not fit
in time to talk to me before the wedding, and that they wanted me to do
the wedding without a premarital counseling session.

I said no.

If I had it to do over again, now, I believe I would probably say yes
to such a situation. But then I said no.

Within a couple of weeks, I was in Dallas at a friend's wedding on
a Saturday night. I needed to be at the church in Central Texas for worship on Sunday morning. Then I was to be back in Dallas for a furniture
mart on Monday morning. After driving through the wee hours of Sunday morning, I made the worship service. Just after Sunday School I
asked one of our three deacons if he felt it would be all right to cancel the
evening service. He said that his wife was ill and he would not be at the
morning worship service, but that it sounded fine to him. But when I
asked the other deacons, everything that had been seething under the
surface came out. I still remember the words of the deacon whose daughter's wedding I had refused to do: "I just don't think you love us."

I did go on to Dallas that afternoon, the evening service cancelled.
As I drove along the long track of interstate highway, the tears stung my
eyes and the voices of anger and threat and sorrow came back over and
over again. That evening the deacons called a congregational meeting in
my absence. Later that night I phoned a family in the church to see how
things were. They told me. I said that my letter of resignation would be
in the mail the next morning.

The Post-Mortem

The post-mortem on this failed pastoral relationship went on for years in
my conscience and in conversations with trusted friends. I blamed the
church at first, then myself, then ministry. For a while I saw myself as a
martyr. Martyrdom is such a comfortable way out and relatively easy to
achieve. But so is self-condemnation. And I tried that way as well. Older,
more experienced ministers talked to me. The issue came up in the
course of a unit of Clinical Pastoral Education I took at Baylor Medical
Center, Dallas. I wanted the problem to be simply dogmatic, cultural,
psychological, anything but what it was at its most basic level, personal
and spiritual.

The congregation wrote a letter to one of my college professors listing doctrinal charges against me, particularly detailing my teachings on Baptism and the Lord's Supper. The professor talked to me and sent me on my way with a qualified blessing. But the issue was not simply a breach of doctrine, of course, it was a breach of relationship.

The pastoral leadership that I provided at that time in my life and ministry was not perceived by this congregation as authentic. Thus, I was powerless. In the end, our official relationship could be dispensed with because the personal relationship between us suffered from a fundamental asunderedness.

What they perceived as genuinely pastoral, I did not fulfill. I should have understood this when some of them said my preaching didn't sound like "preaching" to them, not like the "real" and "spiritual" revival preaching of days gone by. The hymns I selected were too distant, too high-sounding, not common to their spiritual repertoire. The worship I led seemed too formal, or at least it seemed not to be comfortable with their style of informality. It lacked the personal directness and warmth they associated with "real" religion.

At that time, and for a long time thereafter, I did not understand the significance of the perception of spiritual and personal authenticity. Without a personal relationship between a minister and a people that is based upon a shared sense of spiritual and personal authenticity, there is no possibility for the constructive use of power or consensus for positive change. Unless a minister perceives as genuine the religious values and directedness of a congregation, and unless a people perceives as genuine the religious life of their minister, the two will remain fundamentally at odds. When, however, they share a sense of religious authenticity, a mutuality of respect and trust concerning the spiritual values and directedness of the other's life, even major differences of policy and goals can be resolved, and positive consensus-based change can be effected.

The question of spiritual authenticity goes to the heart of our common life, to the heart of our celebration of the sacraments and proclamation of the Word. But I discovered this when my early failure as a minister was contrasted against later experiences in which congregations and I shared a common sense of spiritual and personal authenticity.

Some Alternatives

During this time I found myself confronted with stark and irreconcilable alternatives in ministerial leadership. I asked myself whether ministry was a matter of coercion in which the minister understands his or her office as that of a change agent who somehow perceives better than the congregation what changes need to be effected and who makes these changes happen by effectively managing the congregation. We have probably all seen this model of ministerial leadership played out with devastating "effectiveness." We have seen ministers of various denominations, of various political and doctrinal labels, who believe they are called to manipulate others to their ends.

As I observed this approach, especially in those early years, it puzzled me. Does this approach reflect, I wondered, the communion of persons that is proclaimed in our celebration of the sacrament of communion, a communion that, in turn, celebrates a variety of gifts given by the Spirit of God for the joy and development of the community? Does this approach mirror the vulnerability of the God who has made Himself known in Jesus of Nazareth? Are we not, as curates, meant to exercise a ruling cure that reflects the ruling cure of Christ?

I observed another alternative that viewed the minister as virtually disengaged from the communal life of the congregation. Again the denominational or doctrinal or political labels did not matter as much as the minister's personal style of ministry. These ministers tended to see themselves as spiritual hermits whose devotional life was an end in itself, and a rather self-absorbed end at that. Rather than understanding the life of contemplation in its relationship to personal and social transformation, they tended to see contemplation merely as inner exploration, often as little more than psycho-devotional.

While I admired and respected this style more than the coercive style, I found it out of touch with parish life. I had to ask myself: How can we hold together our spiritual authenticity with our practical leadership? And from where does this spiritual authenticity spring? Does it not come from our contemplation of the Triune God whose very Being is in communion? Thus does not spiritual authenticity assume a balance between the inner and the outer life of the spirit, between solitude and community?[1]

A third approach I observed was a passive development of what we often call the "enabler" model. The minister was said to "facilitate" action by organizing the *laos*. But there tended to be a sort of atrophy that developed in many congregations having this model of ministerial leadership, an atrophy in which ministers justified their lack of attentiveness to the details of ministry by saying that their purpose was merely to equip others to do the work, when equipping was viewed virtually as a passive response to lay demand.

This was certainly not satisfying though I found myself tending rather more toward this model than to others. I have come more and more to believe in the ability of people to generate a social or group energy that sees far more possibilities than any single designated "leader." But I had to ask myself whether it is likely for a group to pop up out of the ground to organize vacation church school. Even the best groups will often need some assistance, some active facilitation, from a leader, a minister or director of Christian education, who enjoys and believes in them and in the task to be accomplished.

Obviously these alternatives, as drawn here, are extreme and limited examples, painted with a broad brush stroke. But as I searched for an appropriate model for ministerial leadership, I was drawn to see models in more extreme, black and white terms. It is often a hazard of questing that we are attracted to extremes rather than to moderation. Only with time did I come to see that good leadership involves directness and sensitivity, one's grounding in a center that will hold in the rush of parish life, and the ability to work well with others, sometimes without seeming to "work" at all.

Preliminary Conclusions

As I emerged from seminary I was fortunate to find a Presbyterian parish in the Dallas suburb of Irving that allowed me, as Associate Minister, the freedom to continue my exploration into appropriate leadership models. But even more important, I found among them a community that accepted my ministry as spiritually and personally authentic. This acceptance of spiritual and personal authenticity followed me into my first solo pastoral ministry in the Presbyterian Church.

Emerging from this personal quest are a number of conclusions that we will present in this study. But the first and essential conclusion to which I have come is this:

--In order for us to serve effectively as ministers in any particular parish, despite the various labels of affiliation we may wear, we must be perceived to be personally and spiritually authentic.

--We also must perceive the persons we serve as sharing in this sense of personal and spiritual authenticity. We must respect their way of being and their way of being faithful.

--And we must share with them a common perception of authenticity. This is the very thing that provides the relational framework in which ministry can take place.

--We need to remain open to adapt to various leadership styles in various situations while remaining true to our center of personal and spiritual authenticity.

--To stray from this center is to lose our authenticity. And if we lose our authenticity, we will not participate in the shared power of communion that is essential to everything we are and everything we do as a Christian church.

The Elements of Authenticity

Three Essential Elements

In our experience there are three essential elements of authenticity: (1) a sharing of perception; (2) a sense of the heart; and (3) competence. As the pastor enters into the life of the parish, and as the congregation interacts with the pastor, they watch and listen to evaluate the minister's performance. The fact that this evaluation is informal, sometimes unconscious, and usually unspoken, does not take away from the fact that the congregation wants to know specifically and concretely whether or not this pastor is authentic.[2]

Authenticity and Shared Perception

"Does she see things the way we see them?" This is the first question. Before a pastor can expect to be heard, believed, and followed as a leader, s/he must be perceived as one who shares with the congregation a common way of viewing the world as a whole.

The concern here is with the big picture. The question is not: "Does she agree with each of us on each and every issue?" This is impossible! But: "Does she see the importance of the things we see as important? Do we share enough common ground to enter into real dialogue?"

There must be a considerable degree of commonality of perception between the pastor and the parish if the pastor is to be regarded as authentic. To put it another way, unless there is a common language within which authenticity can be communicated, the parishioners will not understand as authentic what the pastor is saying.

This is obviously true in the case of a pastor starting up in a new parish. When I came to the small Central Texas parish the people quickly discerned that I did not see things as they did. My view of the world was not their view of the world.

We are not talking about a right and a wrong view of the world here. We are talking about different perceptions of the world, different perspectives on the whole, which, of course, result in different ways of valuing.

When people look at the new pastor and say, "She doesn't see things the way we see them," it is easy for them to take the next step to say, "She doesn't value what we value."

This is why, in our experience, it is a matter of great importance for clergy to be matched with parishes that share a similar perceptual orientation. Many problems pastors get into in their new parishes derive from perceptual differences that spin off into value related differences.

For example: Susan has recently come to Grace Lutheran Church, an Evangelical Lutheran church in a community of about 7,000. The church was attracted to her initially because of her winsome good humor and her high energy level. Several members of the congregation said that she is just what Grace Church has needed, a real shot in the arm. But now that she is in full swing, there is a growing pocket of animosity toward her.

Susan is hardly ever in her study. The previous pastor (who had been there for fifteen years) was generally to be found in his study unless he was making home or hospital visits. The congregation viewed this as appropriate and enjoyed being able to find the pastor in his customary place.

Susan, however, spends the overwhelming majority of her time out and about in the town, going to various meetings, popping by the

schools, and serving on committees in the larger Church. She has installed an answering phone to take messages.

The murmuring among the congregation is that Susan is never
"working" but is "off gallavanting around." They view the answering
device as impersonal and many times refuse to leave a message. Resent-
ment is growing. Sadly, Susan doesn't even know it yet.

Susan's perception of ministry is active. She works very hard. Yet
she is getting a reputation for being lazy. She sees herself as very available, available indeed throughout the community. But some people are
seeing her as the very opposite. The problem is perceptual.

And the problem is critical. It directly affects the congregation's
estimation of Susan as a pastor. There is a tendency not to perceive her
as authentic because her understanding of ministry is bumping up against
theirs. The problem can be solved. But it can only be solved if she and
they become aware of the nature of the informal evaluation of her authenticity that is going on. In Susan's case, the perceptual gap is probably not too broad to span by means of negotiation and sensitivity. But if
it is left as it is, it will likely only become worse.

Of course, this isn't simply a matter of concern for pastors starting
up in new parishes. Take Martin, for example, the rector of St. Aidan's
Church. St. Aidan's is located in an affluent suburb. Martin came to St.
Aidan's a few years after he left seminary.

At that time he understood his role as being a strategist for social
justice. He was active in a variety of projects in the best tradition of
liberal Protestantism. He was on the board of the community mental
health organization. He worked with planned parenthood organizations.
He enlisted volunteers to march in civil rights demonstrations. He was
active in international justice organizations and in interfaith cooperation
programs. Martin was perceived generally by the St. Aidan congregation
as being a dynamic agent for social justice. And because he and the congregation shared a similar vision, they viewed him as personally and
spiritually authentic.

All went well for several years. But during this time Martin was
rethinking his vocation. He gradually came to feel that his work as a
social strategist lacked sacramental depth. His reflections led him to
move toward a different pastoral approach and even to distance himself
from certain aspects of his previous pastoral work.

Martin, in all of this, sensed a profound spiritual renewal. The congregation, however, experienced a profound sense of dislocation.

They began to ask: "Who is the real Martin?"

Martin saw himself as growing and deepening as a priest. The congregation saw him as shrinking back into an interior piety. They were especially distressed when he gave up involvement in such programs as planned parenthood because he said his views on abortion were changing.

The conflict between Martin and the parish is not simply over opinions about specific issues. It is a fundamental conflict over ways of perceiving the whole of life. Certain changes are predictable in the life of people and organizations. Sometimes a pastor and a congregation change in the same ways and grow in the same direction. Sometimes they may not.

In this situation, Martin has come to view himself as more authentic, personally and spiritually. But the congregation has come to view him as much less so. The problem is perceptual.

Most pastoral situations will not be so starkly contrasted as are these two. In the majority of parishes there are nuances of perception, varieties of ways of looking at the whole of life and faith.

What is essential to understand, however, is this: **The pastor cannot be viewed as personally or spiritually authentic unless s/he and the parishioners share some common perceptual ground.**

Authenticity and a Sense of the Heart

Jonathan Edwards, the American colonial theologian, described true Christianity as being grounded in the "sense of the heart." What he described was a quality of life and Christian faith in which the head and the heart work together. In our experience, authenticity is directly related to the pastor's "sense of the heart."

Not long after coming to our present parish I was visiting with a member of the congregation who persisted in calling me "Dr. Jinkins" after I had frequently asked her to call me Michael. One day while visiting at her house, I again asked her to call me Michael, whereupon she said, "After we get to know you and can see that you live like you have learned, then we will call you Michael."

She was waiting to see if my head and my heart worked together. She was waiting to see if I was the genuine article.

This is one of the most frustrating parts of starting up a new pastoral ministry. Starting up means starting over when it comes to authenticity. Authenticity is not like a bank account we can move with us from parish to parish. In each new parish the clergyperson must be known all over again. S/he must be seen as one who can be trusted in concrete pastoral situations.

Closely related to this connection of head and heart is the sense of personal concern. The question that is running through the minds of parishioners (and that is sometimes asked directly of the new pastor) is this: "Do you like us?"

What is being asked is so simple it is sometimes overlooked. "Do you like us as we are?" But this question is so important it can only be overlooked at the risk of doing the relationship serious harm. The pastor who is regarded as personally authentic is the pastor who accepts the congregation in its uniqueness.

The clergyperson's ability to accept the congregation in its uniqueness is not unrelated to his acceptance of himself. The pastor who is forever attempting to prove himself is unlikely to be very accepting of others.

This is particularly evident in, for instance, a pastor who was reared in a socioeconomic stratum to which he has become unaccustomed following four years of college and three years of graduate school. Suppose that such a pastor is called to a blue collar church, but soon finds his parishioners embarrassingly reminiscent of his own humble background. Neither he nor the members of his congregation are likely to feel comfortable. Unless he is able to come to terms with his own internal conflict and unless he is able to accept his people and love them as they are, he will not be perceived as either personally or spiritually authentic.

Theologians often discuss the importance of consistency between God's being and God's activity. They say that unless God reveals the divine essence through God's particular economic acts, specifically through the incarnation, there is profound uncertainty concerning the being of God. The antidote to such uncertainty is the Church's teaching concerning divine revelation: When by faith we see Jesus Christ, through the power of the divine Spirit, we are looking into the very heart of the Father.

A congregation's concern for the authenticity of the pastor parallels this basic theological teaching. "Is this pastor, *in essentia*, as s/he appears to be in his or her actions?" "Can we count on him to be as he seems to be?" "Does she really feel about us the way she seems to feel?"

Central to the pastoral vocation is the conception of "betrothal." There is a way of being which is truth, and only on this basis can people come together with any sense of promise. A relationship not based on "betrothal" is on shaky ground because the people may not be as they seem to be.

Sissela Bok sets the tone for her remarkable study of mendacity with a quote from St. Augustine: "When regard for truth has been broken down or even slightly weakened, all things will remain doubtful."[3]

As the Seventh Thane of Rothiemurchus in our faerie tale discovered, when we disregard the truthfulness of vocation, we risk the loss of the secret healing voice. I discovered this in my first parish. We easily become lost in a web of vocational inauthenticity when our lives no longer ring true to the ears of our parishioners.

Authenticity and Competence

A friend of ours who directs the department of pastoral counseling services at a university once told us that the biggest single factor in the success of pastoral counseling, in his own experience, is the perception of the client that the counselor is competent.

Competency is essential to authenticity. A question that is asked over and over by parishioners is: "Does this person know what s/he is doing?"

Competence is a large issue. It embraces not only technical concerns, such as hermeneutics, homiletics, doctrinal and liturgical competence, but also intimate issues, such as spiritual direction and personal integrity. If the pastor is found to be incompetent, s/he is unlikely to be perceived as personally and spiritually authentic despite how likeable s/he may be because authenticity assumes capability and not simply amiability.

The motto of the University of Aberdeen was chosen by its founder Bishop Elphinstone in the late fifteenth century. It appears on gateways and arches and tombs and heraldic shields here and there all around the University. The motto reads: "*Initium Sapientiae Timor Domini.*"

"The beginning of wisdom is the fear of the Lord." (Psalm 111:10) The bishop knew his Psalter. But he also knew human nature. Competence in pastoral ministry assumes not only theoretical knowledge but practical understanding as well, and this sort of wisdom is possible only as the result of spiritual discipline.

For several years now we have worked closely with ministers who have recently finished seminary and moved on to parishes. Very often we find them moving through a series of stages as they are stunned initially by the way parishes work, then are angry at their seminaries for not preparing them for the way parishes work, sometimes blaming their seminaries for the conflicts they are having, until finally, gradually, they accept the preparation their seminaries gave them, understanding the limitations of their seminaries and their own responsibility to seek training in practical ministry.

One vocational counselor who works closely with clergy in crisis drew the picture clearly when he commented that the seminaries are just there to give the pastor some basic skills in theology. Unfortunately, as he observed, the parishes are not going to judge the pastor's competence primarily in terms of his or her ability to perform well the skills that the seminary imparts. Rather they are going to judge the pastor much more on the basis of his or her people skills.

While this comment does not take into account changes in many seminary programs and is perhaps one-sided, it does reflect a common perception among many church members that they are meeting newly ordained pastors who are generally good when it comes to talking about the "theoretical," but not as competent when it comes to the "practical business" of pastoral ministry. After decades of talk about this problem it is still a problem.

But what is the "practical business" of pastoral ministry? What is the nature of the wisdom that the minister is to seek?

In observing clergy who are generally perceived by their lay persons as competent, we have gathered informally and totally unscientifically a few general impressions. There are two overlapping areas of competence: professional and interpersonal, both of which depend on the minister's spiritual competence.

This is where the words of the Psalmist via Bishop Elphinstone connect for us. Our professional and interpersonal competence derive from a prior competence, the competence of the spirit. The pastor's competence is either pastoral or it is irrelevant.

This is something of what Joseph Sittler meant when he said, "The principal work of the ordained ministry is reflection: cultivation of one's penetration into the depth of the Word so that the witness is poignant and strong."[4]

Professional competence does not rest in our keeping up with the latest gimmicks of managerial training. Interpersonal competence does not lie in our being able to rattle away in the trendiest psychobabble. Certainly we should seek wisdom wherever it is to be found, but wisdom begins in the awe of God. And only from a spirit nurtured in the depths of a personal struggle with God can a competence emerge that will serve the pastor and his or her people.

Parishioners do generally expect the pastor to be open to new developments in management and counseling. But, much more, they expect their pastor to serve them as a sacramental leader, a person practiced in the presence of God.

Several years ago a quote from Richard John Neuhaus's book *Freedom For Ministry* appeared on the cover of *The Presbyterian Outlook*. Neuhaus wrote:

> Any ministry that finds its authority in contemporary notions of professionalism is on perilous ground indeed. Yet the walls of many clergy offices are littered by diplomas and certificates from academic institutions and professional associations. It is a pitiable imitation of the doctor's office, where diplomas are designed both to intimidate the patients into accepting doctor's orders and to assure them that they are in good hands. One should not try to intimidate the people of God, especially with something that is finally so trivial as academic diplomas. Perhaps the pastor might hang up a piece of paper certifying that he has achieved a certain level of holiness and spiritual discernment, but the institution that could issue such certification has yet to be found. It is bad enough that one should try to intimidate or even impress parishioners with such shoddy evidence of authorization. What is much worse is that the minister himself might derive his sense of authority from such evidence. The appeal to the appurtenances of professionalism is a poignant confession of vocational bancruptcy.... If the wall of the pastor's office is to make a declaration worthy of the calling, let it

display a simple cross or crucifix. That, finally, is all we have to say for ourselves.[5]

I clipped that cover and had it framed, and for years it hung on the wall of my study beside my own diplomas and certifications. These hung there together in complete incongruity until recently I decided that I ought to take down either the Neuhaus quote or my diplomas. I kept the Neuhaus quote and put my diplomas in a drawer.

Our professional competence and our interpersonal competence do not derive from external or secondary sources of authorization. They derive from a competence of the spirit. And no matter how our particular parishes define that quality of competence (and they do define it variously depending upon cultural, social, denominational, and theological differences), our parishioners demand this competence as a prerequisite of authenticity.

An Authentic Power

John Fletcher in his monograph on religious authenticity made the critical judgment: "My observation is that congregations hold the power to authenticate ("make real") the person and work of the clergy, even in denominations with hierarchical structures and episcopally defined ordination policies."[6]

The issue of authenticity is crucial to the exercise of pastoral ministry. Those who are perceived as authentic have the power to get things done. Those who are not are powerless to make a difference.

Authenticity, as we have seen, is a communal dynamic. That is, a pastor is discerned by others to be or not to be authentic. One's authenticity is established in actual, concrete relationships with other persons. As we shall see in the following chapter, this is also true of pastoral authority and personal power. The pastor and the parish establish the boundaries of ministerial power so the pastor's "cure of souls" can never be something he holds in his or her own hands as though it were private property. But we shall better understand this as we turn now to consider the interrelationship of power and authority in pastoral ministry.

NOTES

1. An especially helpful discussion of this balance of interior and exterior life, of solitude and community, is to be found in Henri Nouwen, *Making All Things New: An Invitation to the Spiritual Life* (San Francisco: Harper & Row, 1981), Chapter III.

2. John C. Fletcher's *Religious Authenticity in the Clergy: Implications for Theological Education* (Washington, DC: The Alban Institute, 1975) is the classic statement on religious authenticity.

3. Sissela Bok, *Lying: Moral Choice in Public and Private Life* (New York: Random House, 1978).

4. Joseph Sittler, *Gravity and Grace: Reflections and Provocations*, Linda-Marie Dellof, editor (Minneapolis: Augsburg, 1986), 49.

5. Richard John Neuhaus, *Freedom for Ministry*, quoted and reviewed in *The Presbyterian Outlook*, Vol. 161 (October 1, 1979), Number 35.

CHAPTER II

Power and Authority

No one presumes to teach an art till he has first, with intent meditation, learned it. What rashness is it, then, for the unskilled to assume pastoral authority, since the government of souls is the art of arts!

—St. Gregory the Great,
The Pastoral Rule

Power and Authority at Work

Andrew serves a suburban church in a large metropolitan center. But before going to this suburban church he had served for several years a much smaller, rural congregation. A perceptive and sensitive pastor, Andrew's reflections are valuable for understanding the relationship between the pastor's power and authority. Realizing, of course, that parishes have different sorts of corporate personalities, we wondered, what are the dynamics of power and authority in these kinds of churches?

In the smaller, rural parish, Andrew said, his ability to get things done, to make changes, to move the church to those goals he believed most important, was directly related to the congregation's understanding of his role as pastor, or to use the old designation in the Presbyterian Church, the role of "teaching elder." "It often felt a lot like the Jewish model of the Rabbi," Andrew explained. As long as he spoke from this teaching, preaching, liturgical, broadly pastoral, caring role, his ideas and plans were given the utmost attention. During the entire time that he served this rural parish (over eight years), there was only one thing he wanted that was not accomplished and even that was given great attention by the ruling board of the church.

And what about the suburban church?

In some ways the case is the same, Andrew said. They seem to respect the pastoral role and to give greater weight to what he has to say, as long as it is directly related to his teaching-preaching-liturgical roles or his role as pastoral counselor. But perhaps, he said, there is less respect for the traditionally broad scope of the pastor's authoritative role.

There is a lot of turnover in a suburban church, he explained, and much of the new growth is from different denominational traditions, even from people who have had little or no Christian education. There's a lot more of the "show me" attitude: Prove to me that this change is justifiable. The rural parish in which he had served was largely a home-grown, lifelong church membership congregation. The move from the first parish to the second had been a jolting experience, especially in relation to the monthly meetings of the governing board of the parish.

He said that he had almost lost his temper several times, because he sensed from some members of the board a suspicion and a lack of trust in him. Much of the trust that seemed built into the previous parish ministry was earned in the second.

Power and Authority

Roy Oswald has distinguished carefully between power and authority while recognizing the link between the two. He writes:

> One definition of authority is role power. Every system assigns specific amounts of authority to individuals occupying roles. They are given enough 'authority' to execute the functions of their roles... Hence the subtle difference between power and authority. Authority is granted to people by the system through roles to be occupied. Power relates to the individuals' ability to accomplish things outside of or above the authority given to them in roles.[1]

Oswald's description of authority and its relation to power certainly fits what we see repeatedly in pastor-parish experience. For instance in Andrew's situation, he has noticed a positive correlation between his ability to get things done and his staying within the boundaries of his role. In the first parish the boundaries of the role were perhaps larger. At one time, the pastor had been regarded as "the first citizen" of the town. Andrew reaped the benefits of the vestiges of this older attitude in his first parish, a smaller, rural church.

Our conversation also revealed that Andrew's sphere of power considerably exceeded his narrower sphere of authority. Over a period of years he had emerged as an important leader in the town and the county. He was widely viewed as a person whose judgment could be trusted, and his compassion was well known. His reputation established him as a significant and powerful person.

When Andrew went to the second parish two things happened that greatly affected his ability to get done those things he felt were important. (1) He entered a parish where the sphere of pastoral authority was somewhat smaller. There were many in the community who had knowledge and experience that seemed analogous, in the eyes of many of the parishioners, to the minister's areas of knowledge and experience. Thus, even those areas where he had experienced an unrivaled sense of authority were intruded upon by others in the helping professions and in management, fundraising, teaching, public speaking, and so forth. He did have a core of pastoral role responsibilities that allowed him to speak with authority, but even this core was strictly limited. (2) He quickly found that the reputational power he had enjoyed, which went far beyond his pastoral role, was not transferred to the new parish. He was not "known" for his good judgment and his compassion. So he found that his critical reflections and advice were not given the consideration to which he had grown accustomed. He sensed this when he said that it seemed he would have to earn the people's trust, something he felt was given to him in the first parish. Actually, the trust he saw as given in the first congregation (and larger community) was not simply given. It also had been earned over a considerable period of time. What had been "given" was the power to make things happen within the boundaries of his authority role as pastor.

Making Some Distinctions

In a remarkable paper written several years ago, Loren Mead charted the actual workings of authority. He distinguished between "five basic types of authority": (1) the authority of knowledge, (2) the authority of expertise, (3) the authority of personal charisma, (4) the authority of 'otherness' (generally referring, in this context, to the pastor's spiritual quality of life), and (5) the authority of role.[2]

In our experience, pastoral authority is essentially the same as the last of these types while the other types tend more to be distinctions of the pastor's power beyond the boundaries of his authoritative role. We have found that the pastoral authoritative role is a discrete sphere which is larger or smaller depending upon the total perceptions of a specific congregation and this congregation's denominational, cultural, and theological traditions. What Mead describes as other "types" of authority are actually separate spheres of power, more or less discrete among themselves, that overlap the authoritative sphere of the pastor. A particular pastor may bring to the authoritative role of pastor certain qualities (of expertise, knowledge, otherness, or charisma) that will enhance his or her authoritative role.

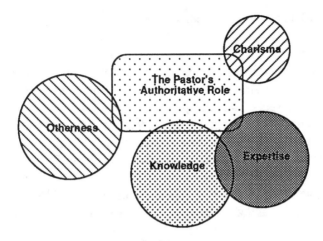

Authority and Personal Power

This relates directly to what we described in Chapter I as authenticity and competence. Parishioners will certainly assume that a particular pastor has some degree of power to fulfill the requirements of the pastoral role. But these types of power should not be identified with the authoritative role of the pastor itself.

In Andrew's case, in his first parish the sphere of pastoral authority consisted of an enlarged role rich in a variety of functions. He was powerful (that is, able to accomplish what he wanted) within the boundaries of this large pastoral sphere simply because he was the pastor. This sphere included preaching, teaching, liturgy, pastoral care and counseling, a great deal of community service, fundraising, and so forth.

In time, as he participated in the life of his congregation and in leadership positions in the town and county, he came to possess a good deal of power beyond his pastoral role. His expertise and knowledge proved valuable in a number of settings. His simple devotion and personal warmth were widely appreciated. The power he accumulated greatly enhanced his pastoral authority.

When Andrew came to his new parish he quickly discovered that the sphere of pastoral authority, the authority "given" by the congregation, was diminished in scope. There were other resident experts in public speaking, counseling, education, even liturgy. He certainly was regarded as an important figure. But not as *the* important figure. That which was distinctively the pastoral role was limited and so was his authority. Within a very small sphere he had the power to get certain things done simply because he was the pastor. But this "given" sphere was very small indeed.

While he experienced a shrinkage of his authoritative role, he experienced initially a virtual disappearance of his other spheres of power, spheres he had largely taken for granted, and had assumed were implicit to his role. His expertise, knowledge, otherness, charisma had to be displayed. They were not presupposed by his congregation.

Andrew experienced a painful early period in his new parish. But, not surprisingly, as the months wore on and the people came to know him better, he found that he was able to get more done. His power increased though the authority he enjoyed by virtue of his pastoral role did not.

Understanding the Instruments and Sources of Power

Before pursuing the subject of authority and the related, but subtlely different, subject of religious authority, it would be wise to consider the way power works via power's instruments and sources. A helpful, though truncated, analysis of power is provided in John Kenneth Galbraith's *The Anatomy of Power*. Galbraith, drawing upon his experience in economics and politics, explains that "there are three instruments for wielding or enforcing" power. "And there are three institutions or traits that accord the right of its use."

The instruments of power are according to Galbraith:

– Condign power: "Condign power wins submission by inflicting or threatening appropriately adverse consequences."

– Compensatory power: "Compensatory power, in contrast, wins submission by the offer of affirmative reward—by giving something of value to the individual so submitting."

– Conditioned power: "Conditioned power, in contrast, is exercised by changing belief. Persuasion, education, or the social commitment to what seems natural, proper, or right causes the individual to submit to the will of another or of others."[3]

"Behind these three instruments for the exercise of power," Galbraith continues, "lie the three sources of power—the attributes or institutions that differentiate those who wield power from those who submit to it. These three sources are personality, property (which, of course, includes disposable income), and organization."[4]

Galbraith's greatest contribution in his analysis of power is not his differentiation between its instruments or its sources. We shall see other more precise descriptions of these. Rather, where Galbraith helps us is in understanding how each source of power relates to the other sources of power and how a particular source of power is best dealt with when one uses a corresponding source.

For instance: Those who have power derived from personality are made more powerful still by the possession of property. When a person has both personal and property power, he or she may add to his or her strength by joining forces with others of like mind.

Property power, Galbraith says, "always exists in association with organization and, not infrequently, with a dominant personality." Power that derives from organization is supported by the possession of property and by dynamic personalities who support the interests of the organization.

"Each source of power, in turn, has a strong, though never exclusive, relationship with a specific instrument of enforcement. Organization is associated with conditioned power: property, needless to say, with compensatory power. Personality has an original and long-standing association with condign power..."[5]

In a corresponding manner, each instrument and source of power is answered or countered by a corresponding instrument and source of power. This is what Galbraith calls the "symmetry" between both the instruments and sources of power and the "countervailing response." Strong personalities call forth the response of strong personalities. These personalities make use of a variety of instruments of power to get what they want, often meeting force with force, sometimes enticing receptive responses with promised rewards, other times attempting to convince others of the benefits of their own designs. The principle that Galbraith describes in considerable detail might be called a "natural principle." That is, Galbraith is seeking to describe what actually happens.

Galbraith's analysis is helpful for those of us in the parish because it is important for us to know what is happening, at whose behest, and why, before we can come to a decision about how we can respond in a measured way in a particular situation. For instance, let us take a purely hypothetical case.

Cynthia is pastor of a new parish. She has been in this congregation for only two months. At meetings of the church board, Cynthia has been impressed by a general sense of comradery. But one particular member of the board has been something of a thorn in Cynthia's flesh. She is another young woman (we'll call her Bernice), a successful accountant, who puts forth her suggestions with enormous energy but with an aggressive edge, as though the rest of the board are stupid or dishonest if they do not agree with her.

Cynthia, at the first meeting of the board, felt attacked by Bernice. And her first response to Bernice's remarks was sharp and defensive. She felt pushed and so she pushed back. Fire drew fire.

Bernice left this first meeting fuming, and so did Cynthia.

Before the next meeting, Cynthia greeted most of the board members warmly. She was, after all, very glad to see them. But Bernice received only a stiff and formal welcome to the meeting. And she knew it.

Before the meeting's agenda was half-through Bernice had an issue to raise. And Cynthia had an answer. The battle lines were drawn. Cynthia used her considerable ability as a communicator to assemble her arguments. Then she used her ability as an organizer and her own personal strength to pull together the agreement of the board members. Within a very short time Bernice was effectively isolated and silenced, but also embarrassed, beaten, and hurt.

From one perspective, the response was natural. And yet the outcome was counterproductive.

The insights we can draw from Galbraith's analysis can help us to understand the dynamics of power in such a way so as to respond intentionally, in a manner that may actually be opposed to our own first tendency.

Another scenario for this situation might have gone like this. Cynthia, knowing that Bernice approaches things with gusto and aggression, might have listened carefully to what Bernice was saying in this second meeting so that Bernice would have felt heard. Then, when Bernice had finished, Cynthia could have asked if the board would mind her going over in detail Bernice's ideas with Bernice at a time when the two of them could sit down alone together. Cynthia would then have had an opportunity to reframe the entire conflict into an event in which Bernice was taken seriously and Cynthia was perceived as both sensitive and open while allowing the board meeting to proceed.

The chances are that such a strategy would achieve two goals: it would allow Cynthia an opportunity to move the discussion on from a potentially harmful direction, and it would allow a personal bond to be established between Cynthia and Bernice. Certainly such a strategy would avoid the alienation of Bernice which we saw in the first scenario. Many pastors have paid dearly for the momentary elation they have gained when they have "won" in a "win-lose" situation. Such perceived "wins" are not in fact wins at all.

The Galbraith model helps in another way also. This model helps us to understand why certain kinds of situations in the parish call upon specific kinds of expertise. Several years ago a church member was explaining to me why clergy should never hold administrative positions for a denomination. "They don't know anything about finances," he said, "because they've never had any real financial training or experience in the business world. What we need in administrative positions are people who are business people." He was saying this after he completely discounted the advice of an administrative officer of a denominational institution who was a clergyperson.

Quite often in board meetings we have observed over the years, budget items have been approved or rejected because a strong personality who has experience in business makes a statement in favor of or in opposition to the items being considered.

We recently heard someone make the statement that there are two things to take into consideration in any issue regarding education: what is the idealistic value and the real economic value of a particular program. Many people make just such a dichotomy in regard to the mission of the church. And those who do will pay particular attention to what those in the real world (that is, the business world) have to say about a purchase or a new program that the church board is considering.

Obviously a prudent pastor might consider spending some time talking with several businesspersons, attempting to build a consensus, or seeking out the support of a highly regarded individual who has considerable experience in finances if he or she is hoping to begin a new program. The endorsement of people acquainted with the distribution and use of property power (including finances) is necessary to establish the validity of a proposal that involves economic issues.

This entire discussion, of course, relates directly back to our consideration of the pastor's sphere of authority. Even in parishes that have a generally broad conception of the pastor's role, few if any conceive of the pastor's role as including much authority in finances. And because financial issues are essential to the life of any organization, the pastor must come to terms with how s/he can exercise responsible power in this area, while recognizing that his or her authority as pastor does not generally extend in this direction.

The most obvious way the pastor can extend his power initially in this area is through communication, what Galbraith called "conditioning." The pastor can help the board understand that there is only one real world and that this world involves financial issues as well as issues involving ideals. The success of new ventures in this area will likely depend upon the building of consensus or the approval of highly respected individuals. In time the pastor may even earn the reputation of being "exceptionally" good with financial matters. But if the pastor moves to another congregation, this particular reputation may not necessarily move with him or her since it is an element in his or her power and not implicit in pastoral authority as it is generally conceived.

The "Powerful" Leader

To give perhaps a more precise understanding of the way power works, let's look at it in a different way. In Paul Hersey and Kenneth Blanchard's modern classic on human resources, they cite the classification system for power bases developed by French and Raven, with the additional insights provided by Kruglanski, who identified the power base of information.

Their system of classification is as follows:

Coercive Power (which is "based on fear");

Legitimate Power (which is "based on the position of the leader");

Expert Power (which is "based on the leader's possession of expertise, skill, and knowledge, which, through respect, influence others");

Reward Power (which is "based on the leader's ability to provide reward for other people");

Referent Power (which is "based on the leader's personal traits");

Information Power (which is "based on the leader's possession of or access to information that is perceived as valuable by others");

Connection Power (which is "based on the leader's 'connections' with influential or important persons inside or outside the organization").[6]

A careful reading of this system of classification reveals that it covers essentially the same ground as the Galbraith analysis, though it is more precise in its distinctions. What is especially helpful in Hersey and Blanchard is their application of this system.

Hersey and Blanchard take these observations directly to the subject of organizational leadership and ask what power base is the best? After carefully accessing original research on this question they conclude that no particular power base is the best in all situations. "In other words," they write, "leaders may need various power bases, depending on the situation."[7]

They do observe, however, a pattern that emerges in the research. The pattern suggests that there is "a direct relationship between the level of maturity of individuals and groups and the kind of power bases that have a high probability of gaining compliance from those people." They define "maturity" as "the ability and willingness of individuals and groups to take responsibility for directing their own behavior in a particular situation." Thus, maturity is not simply, in their usage of the word, a quality of character that applies universally to all situations, but is "a task-specific concept and depends on what the leader is attempting to accomplish."[8]

The seven bases of power, in Hersey and Blanchard's observations, seem to have correspondingly "significant impact on the behavior of people" depending upon the "various levels of maturity." In other words, a group of people who involved in a particular situation have "low maturity" (that is, who fail "to take responsibility for directing their own behavior") will respond best to coercive power (power based on fear, perhaps fear of particular and very specific undesirable results from the consequences of failure). On the other hand, a group of people who involved in a particular situation have a high degree of maturity (that is, who are willing "to take responsibility for directing their own behavior") might be anticipated to respond favorably to the "expert power" base.

Hersey and Blanchard provide the following chart to illustrate this correlation: "The impact of power bases at various levels of maturity."

High Maturity

Expert
Information
Referent
Legitimate
Reward
Connection
Coercive

Low Maturity

Following the insights of Hersey and Blanchard we might say that a committee that has "low maturity" (according to the situational definition of Hersey and Blanchard) will need strong direction in order to accomplish its goals. A person who is a bit more mature may respond well to a less directive model of leadership, perhaps based on connectional or reward power bases. Someone with a moderate level of maturity may respond well to the leader because the leader has become legitimized in his or her perception. A person or a group in the moderate to higher level of maturity tends to need comparatively little direction, but they need significant amounts of communication and support from the leader, available via a "referent power" base. Those who are higher yet in their maturity level respond especially well to participatory and delegating forms of leadership. They appreciate the kind of leadership that relies on an "information power" base because they are looking to the leader for information in order to maintain or improve their performance of a task. Finally, those who possess a high level of maturity in a given circumstance usually require little direction or support. They are both able and willing to perform the tasks required and to respond most readily to delegating. The leader is looked to by these more for the leader's competence and confidence than for specific directions at every step of the way.[9]

What stands out in this analysis of the workings of power in groups is that a good leader needs to be flexible. A good leader allows the needs of those she is leading to shape her style of leadership. This came as a particular surprise to me (Michael) several years ago when attending a leadership conference.

Having been an avid student of church administration in seminary, I approached the conference with a certain amount of confidence that I knew pretty much anything the leader of the conference had to teach me. During the course of the conference I was tested on my "style" of leadership.

In seminary I had learned the importance of delegation, of being a facilitator for others to do the ministry of the church. What I did not understand was that this model alone is not enough.

When I read the results of my test, I discovered that in roughly fifty per cent of the situations I was faced with, I had not led in a manner likely to get the best response. Some situations called for a leader who would be very directive, others for a leader who would help people to do their tasks by providing an example. Some situations called for a leader who could clearly show the condign consequences that would befall those who did not tackle the task. Other situations called for merely a hint of a suggestion that if we accomplished our goal a wonderful reward awaited us.

I consistently followed one model of leadership. What I had not yet discerned was that life is not so consistent as to respond to a single model of leadership, however good that particular model may be. Good leadership has to follow the contours of life and be custom-made to fit new and different situations.

A separate but related question that confronts us in light of Hersey and Blanchard's analysis of power has to do with the relationship of power and authority. What we have referred to as the authoritative role of the pastor corresponds roughly to what Hersey and Blanchard understand as "Legitimate Power." This is the power based "on the position of the leader." As we shall see, there are other factors in the pastor's authority that make this entire scheme a good deal less exact. But, for the moment, let us concentrate on this one factor.

If the pastoral sphere of authority, the pastor's role as pastor, is what corresponds to "Legitimate Power," and if a pastor leans primarily on his or her pastoral authority as a power base, his or her power will be significantly limited.

Part of what we are saying is simply a statement of fact, a fact that we have already noticed in Andrew's situation. Andrew's power, based on his pastoral authority, was greater in the small, rural parish because his sphere of pastoral authority (those areas in which he was considered authoritative) was more inclusive. Add to the power Andrew gained in other areas beyond his strictly pastoral role, and Andrew was very powerful (that is, he could get a lot done) in the first parish.

But, as we have seen, when he moved to the suburban parish, Andrew's power diminished considerably. The power beyond his role did not move with him. And the sphere of pastoral authority based upon his role as pastor was considerably smaller. For some time until he proves himself, this core of pastoral authority derived from the "givens" of his pastoral role will be virtually all Andrew has in terms of effective power.

Andrew will need to be very intentional about his use of power bases if he wants to make things happen as a leader. The "Legitimate Power," as we have seen in Hersey and Blanchard, is most effective in situations where people operate with a moderate level of maturity. But what if a board, committee, or individual with whom Andrew is working operates at a much lower level of maturity in relation to the particular task facing them? We may anticipate that in such situations Andrew will have to prove himself able to work outside the boundaries of his pastoral role. And, of course, Andrew is able to do this, because quite unknown to himself he has been doing it for years, although he had assumed that most of his power was related to the "givens" of pastoral authority. Identifying the fact that he has successfully performed beyond the boundaries of pastoral authority in the past should be a very positive discovery for Andrew, one that will provide him more confidence in this difficult time of transition. He has the ability to allow his expertise and knowledge, his connections and networking with other professionals, and his interpersonal insights to enhance his pastoral authority and build solid power bases beyond his strictly pastoral role.

Trying To Do the Right Thing:
Two Parenthetical Remarks

Dr. Louis Adams, director of the Pastoral Counseling Center at the Brite Divinity School, Texas Christian University, recently told us something that is one of the hardest things to remember when you are in the heat of pastoral leadership encounters. He said you have to remember that most people in the congregation are just trying to do what they think is the best thing. Their motives are essentially altruistic. Based upon their understanding of their own highest self-interests, the interests of those about whom they are most concerned, what they think best for the church, their concerns for the larger community, and their perception of you as the pastor, they are acting in the way they believe will be best.

We have found this insight very helpful in clarifying why some people do not want to take responsibility for achieving a particular goal in a particular situation. The important thing to remember, as Louis explains it, is that the individual may be unwilling to commit to the task the leader wants accomplished because he or she has not understood the task as contributing to the good of the group or to his or her own good.

Another factor related to this concern has to do with those persons who are unable to contribute to the task because they do not know how to act appropriately. Frequently, a leader may assume that all members of the group have the ability to take responsibility for the completion of a particular task, when some members of the group may not know how. This we have seen, in particular, in relation to recruiting and stewardship programs. Some persons who view either of these tasks as important may feel unable to contribute to the achievement of the task. A pastor who relies primarily on nondirective leadership may not see the goals of such a program attained simply because he or she has assumed too much on behalf of the parishioners involved.

The Authority of the Curate

So far we have been talking about power and authority in most any human group. Corporations deal with much the same dynamics. So do schools. So do government agencies. But there are other dynamics at work in the pastor-parish relationship.

Pastors are, as St. Gregory the Great elegantly expressed it, "physicians of the heart." And to exercise the cure of hearts, he says, one must have a thorough understanding of "spiritual precepts."

As we said before, the cure of souls includes both a ruling and a healing cure. But how does this cure work? What is happening when the pastor exercises his or her pastoral authority? Is this a matter that can be understood in purely naturalistic terms? Or is something else going on?

Loren Mead raised these questions in the short paper we referred to in the beginning of this chapter. He is aware that the subject he is raising is a messy one. "I think," he writes, "that when we talk about religious authority we are talking about a different dimension, if not a different animal."

He continues:

In some sense I suspect that the parishioner, sitting in the study with his or her pastor, is engaged in working out some very deep things in relationship with the only authority with real dependability, with God. . . . [I]n sofar as I am perceived to be a pastor, that person facing me lays important, sometimes very tender, defensive or fearful projections upon me, not because of who I am but because of an authority he or she imputes to me as bearer of a mystery . . . More and more . . . I am beginning to see this murky issue to be the heart of the authority question for the pastor. In what way does the pastor become a resource to people who are working out their issues with God in their transactions with the pastor? . . . You see, as I told Terry Holmes the other day, when you quit talking about 'authority' and start talking about 'religious authority,' 'It's like shifting from playing tic-tac-toe to playing three-dimensional chess![10]

Authority, as we have been describing it, is directly related to the pastor's role. But at the heart of the pastor's authority is the mystery with which Loren is grappling. Attempts to understand this essentially "religious" dynamic of pastoral authority in terms of "transference" are only partially satisfactory. Certainly the pastor confronts transference among those he or she meets, for better or for worse. In a variety of environments, including but not limited to pastoral counseling, people may transfer their feeling for another (a previous pastor, an old friend, a relative, perhaps even their notions about God) to the pastor. This is an element in what is happening, but it is a relatively superficial element. There is something more essential at work (and we are consciously using the term in its narrower and more technical sense: essential, having to do with the essence—the being—of the pastor as a person called by God into the ministry of the Word and sacraments). And this something more essential is not simply restricted to the parishioner's perception of the pastor, but is dependent upon the pastor's own personal vocation.

Loren is much closer to the murky depths of this mystery when he relates the "religious authority" of the pastor to the theology of the Word and the sacraments. But, as he said, to deal with this issue we must move well beyond the convenient and neat treatment of the subject. And as we do, we find that the pastor's religious authority has to do only secondarily with the perceptions of his or her parish.

The pastor's religious authority is grounded primarily in Christ's pastoral office, in which the pastor participates by the power of the Spirit. In a sense, then, even pastoral counseling is a participation in the life of the Trinity. The parishioner is drawn to see his or her life more clearly, more critically, yet more graciously. The pastor facilitates this clarity of vision in such a way that the parishioner may sense that he or she is working out his or her problems in the presence of God through the mediation of one who serves as "priest." But the "priesthood" of the pastor is derived from the "high priesthood" of Christ, who bears into the presence of God, through the Spirit of Truth and Love, the humanity of humanity (the humanity of both the parishioner and the pastor) and who communicates the grace and judgment of God to and through humanity in his own personhood.

The pastor's authority as curate, as we indicated in the introduction, does not simply derive from the people's subjective response to him or her or even to the office of pastor. These factors are important to our consideration. But they are not the essential factor. What is essential is the curacy of Christ himself, who defines, realizes, and fulfills the Cure of all souls and in whom we, as pastors, participate, by the power of the Spirit of Christ, in our cure. The authority of the pastoral office is sacramental in all its expressions, not merely in liturgy. The Word incarnates Himself through the medium of the whole pastoral office so that pastors may serve God's healing purpose as participants in the Curacy of Christ.

This is the theological center from which the pastor works, not primarily his or her personal "style," not merely his or her knowledge or accumulation of resources, nor simply his or her networking with other professionals. All of these other elements that relate to the pastor's various power bases have their place, but they are all at the disposal of the pastor under the critical judgment of his or her participation in the Curacy of Christ.

A particular congregation may view the pastor's authoritative role in more limited terms. An individual parishioner may transfer feelings of anger or regret to the pastor as the representative of God. A pastor may find himself or herself operating outside the boundaries of his or her pastoral role. But in all things, the pastor's doing and being has its authoritative grounding in the Curacy of Christ—beyond all subjective interpretations—and it is in light of this high Curacy that the pastor's entire ministry is to be lived out.

Pastoral Authority in the Big Picture

The practical result of these insights into the ground of pastoral authority is that we, as pastors, are freed to utilize many tools and styles of leadership, to avail ourselves of a variety of managerial programs, to act from any number of power bases, and to do so with remarkable freedom, but to do so always in light of the Curacy of Christ, Christ's own pastoral ministry in which we participate through the Spirit of God. What happens practically is that the pastor is responsible to reflect upon the uses of his or her authority and power, to determine whether they express the goals and concerns consistent with the pastoral office as a participation in Christ's cure of souls. Even on the most practical level, at a deacons' meeting, in a communicants' class, or in the middle of a building program, the pastor is acting with an authority that is given by virtue of this essential participation in the pastoral ministry of Christ, even while s/he is aware of the interpersonal or systemic dynamics of authority and power.

Thus Andrew or our hypothetical Cynthia will be conscious of the essential connectedness of their pastoral ministry to the ministry of Christ. And conscious of this real sacramental connection, they will allow their pastoral authority to be shaped by the source of their authority.

Mead has said that this is a messy business, and he is right in that the religious authority of the pastor is not easily treated in neat lists and classification systems. And yet anyone who has served long as a pastor is aware of a level of dynamics that operates much deeper than the purely organizational. Perhaps this is why in the past decade we have seen among Protestant pastors as well as Roman Catholic priests a phenomenal increase of interest in the writings of Thomas Merton and Henri Nouwen, both of whom indicate that the heart of our vocation lies in the objective Being of the Trinity and not simply in our subjective perceptions, important as these perceptions are.

Understanding something of the ground of our authority and its communal dynamics, we are ready, finally, to address the issue of change in the parish. But as we do so, we are not leaving behind the theological aspects of our reflection to descend (as it were) to the practical. In fact, it would be wise to begin with a consciously theological reflection so that our discussion of change and control can be framed appropriately.

NOTES

1. Roy Oswald, *Power Analysis*, 7.

2. Loren B. Mead, "Authority and Religious Authority," *Action Information*, The Alban Institute, December, 1976, 1-4.

3. John Kenneth Galbraith, *The Anatomy of Power* (Boston: Houghton Mifflin Company, 1983), 4-6. Reprinted by permission of Houghton Mifflin Company. Roy Oswald's excellent monograph *Power Analysis of a Congregation* provides a similar description of the dynamics of power. Oswald also provides the most helpful instrument for the analysis of the instruments of power in a congregation, pages 9-12 of *Power Analysis*.

4. Ibid., 6.

5. Ibid., 38-39.

6. Paul Hersey and Kenneth H. Blanchard, *Management of Organizational Behavior: Utilizing Human Resources* (Englewood Cliffs, NJ: Prentice-Hall, Inc., Fourth edition, 1982), 178-179.

7. Ibid., 181.

8. Ibid., 181.

9. Ibid., 182-184. Our summary here of Hersey and Blanchard is brief indeed. Their own work bears looking at with considerable care.

10. Loren B. Mead, "Authority and Religious Authority," 3-4.

CHAPTER III

Power, Control, and Change

The ultimate end of our pastoral oversight is that which is the ultimate end of our whole lives; even the pleasing and glorifying of God, and the glorification of His Church.

—Richard Baxter,
The Reformed Pastor

Before examining the research available to us on the subject of power, control, and change, it will be helpful to reflect intentionally from a theological perspective on the contrast between power and control. Many of the issues with which we will deal in this theological reflection will meet us in a variety of practical contexts in the following sections.

Theological Reflections on Power and Control

There is a kind of power that empowers others, and there is a kind of power that seeks to control others by limiting their power. There is no end to illustrations of the latter kind of power. But there is in the Christian tradition an especially helpful description of the former. The kind of power that empowers is best observed in the Day of Pentecost, as the Church came into being, receiving power when the Holy Spirit came upon it.[1]

The curate's power, speaking in a strictly theological frame, is to be exercised in a manner consistent with (and indeed flowing from) God's own sharing of power in and through the Church, a sharing of power that is defined by the entire movement of God toward humanity in the Incarnation and Pentecost. Beginning in the Magnificat, we are struck by the unexpectedness of God's power, which sets the world's powers on end. Though we have recounted the stories a thousand times, the birth of Christ, the life of Christ, the death of Christ, even the resurrection of Christ, surprise us when we reflect upon them as the unveiling of God's power.

And so when we come to the day of Pentecost, and we are told that the Church is being *empowered* by the Holy Spirit, this does not mean that persons are manipulated and grasped so that they may manipulate and grasp other persons, but that they are given power to free persons from manipulation and grasping. The power given is essentially the same power that was in Jesus Christ who died for others, yet who in his death overpowered the powers of death.

Power as a merely creaturely thing can be used in bad or good ways for bad or good purposes. But power that reflects the God who empowers by the Holy Spirit, by definition, reflects the qualities (Love, Truth, and Life) of the One who shares the power. The power of God, to put it another way, is given through the Holy Spirit so that we may participate in the character of Christ.

The reason we must reflect on power intentionally from a theological perspective, as we are doing just now, is that pastors commonly feel so uncomfortable speaking of power at all. Most pastors, like most people, regard power with great suspicion. They generally agree with Lord Acton's axiom: *"Power tends to corrupt and absolute power corrupts absolutely."*[2]

As in many popular aphorisms there is some truth in Lord Acton's words. But as in many aphorisms, truth suffers for pithiness of phrase. Power can be used corruptly, but it is doubtful that it is power itself that tends toward the corruption.

Gregory Bateson has called this bit of popular wisdom enshrined in Lord Acton's words "nonsense." "What is true," he wrote, "is that the *idea of power* corrupts."[3] On the basis of our experience, we would agree with Bateson.

Power itself is the ability to get things done, as we have said before. But there is a seductiveness about the idea of power, especially the *idea* of power as the power to subdue. There is a virtual mythology of power *as control,* as the ability to get one's own way at the expense of others. Elias Canetti, the Nobel Prize winning writer, has analyzed the exercise of power *as control,* in terms of seizing and incorporating, using the image of physical consumption as the appropriate metaphor for understanding the subduing of others for one's own gain.[4] Those who are seduced by the *idea* of power and who tend to identify themselves and their endeavors with the *mythology* of power (that is, imagining themselves as members of an elite power cult who are Masters over all others), also tend to seek power for the sake of controlling the behavior of others.

The contrast between power as control and power as empowering is displayed vividly in C.S. Lewis' excursion into the world of "devils," *The Screwtape Letters.* A professional devil, Screwtape, giving instructions to the apprentice, Wormwood, explains that to the devils "a human is primarily food." "Our aim is the absorption of its will into ours, the increase of our own area of selfhood at its expense." But, he explains, "the Enemy" (the devils' enemy, God) seeks to empower humans to live freely as God's children. Such an idea is loathsome to Screwtape. He continues, "We want cattle who can finally become food; He [God] wants servants who can finally become sons."[5]

Bateson also reminds us that power is necessarily systemic. This applies alike to power as an empowering liberation and power as a controlling force.

Power as an empowering liberation of persons is communal. Persons are freed, in a sense, to utilize their gifts, their personal abilities and perspectives, for the greater good of the whole "Body." The members of the "Body" contribute freely for the sake of the whole as they draw their life-force and direction from the "Head of the Body," Christ. They find themselves in communion to be transformed so that they can enjoy a share in the character of Christ through the communication of the Spirit. But in this transformation and this sharing in the character of Christ, they become more (not less) uniquely themselves.

Power as a controlling and limiting force is also systemic, but systemic in a way that mocks the communal life. The many are manipulated and controlled by the few who usurp the place of "Headship." The many people in the system are used by the few. Rather than freely expressing their gifts, they are assigned functions and are limited to the performance of these functions on the basis of predetermined criteria. Thus, conformity-to-criteria replaces personhood-in-communion.[6]

Thus the fear of power that many pastors feel is not wholly unjustified. But it is misplaced. What we as pastors should fear is not the exercise of power, but the seductive idea of power as control and the various mythologies of power that entice us to forsake the liberation of persons for communal life for the sake of self-glorification.

We shall explore other aspects of control, more and less malevolent, in the following sections as we also track the relationship of the pastor and parish in a specific case. But for now we observe that potential of power for good and for evil, realizing that an adequate understanding of power's potential is possible only in a theological frame.

By observing power in this theological frame, we can understand why many Churches utilize a polity that provides a system with two features: (1) a formal covenantal relationship between the leadership of the parish and the parishioners at large and (2) a system of checks and balances by which power is moderated. The covenantal relationship recognizes God as the ultimate source for power as empowering and the sharing of power as a positive factor in the life of a congregation. Persons enter into covenant, into an unconditional relationship that recognizes the uniqueness of persons with a variety of gifts, and the responsibility of persons to act for the good of the whole. The system of checks and balances recognizes the tendency of persons to use power for the sake of those interests that seem good to them (based upon their own perception of self-interest and the ultimate good of the community), which needs to be checked and balanced by the (often conflicting) perceptions of others in the group. The ideal of the checks and balances of the system is to provide an expression in a group's polity of the variety of individual gifts and perspectives, while attempting to look beyond the particular to the whole. The assumption behind such polities is that power is best exercised when it is exercised dialectically and dialogically.

Differentiating between Control and Change in the Pastoral Environment

Having mapped the contours of power and control from a theological perspective, let us turn our attention to a specific pastor-parish relationship. And as we reflect on this situation, let us broaden our focus considerably beyond the specific concerns that have faced us in the preceding theological reflection. Up until now we have looked at power and control, attempting to understand in fairly bold relief some differences between the two. In real life situations, however, bold relief is rare.

When we are looking at a real life situation in our own parishes, a variety of concerns present themselves in a rich and often contradictory fashion. In the following situation, which has been fictionalized to protect the identity of those involved, we are looking not only at concerns of power and control and change, but also at a number of other concerns such as church size and ministry style, leadership concerns, and questions regarding shifting roles for professional clergy and for the laity as well. These issues often present themselves in surprising ways. Thus, we are not using the situation simply to illustrate the interrelationship of power, control, and change or to demonstrate a particular interpretation of control, though these concerns will certainly arise along the way. Rather, we are attempting to use an actual ministry situation to sharpen our skills at reading life as pastors.

Linda has served as pastor of the Grace Presbyterian Church for about four weeks. Grace Church is a congregation of about 325 members in a small Midwestern town about seventy miles from a large metropolitan center. In those four weeks she has experienced both warmth and generosity from the people, but she is also involved in a crisis of leadership at this point, only a month into her pastorate there.

The previous pastor, a man, served this parish for almost twenty years. He came directly from seminary to the parish. His four children were all born there. His wife was a highly visible, very active, and much loved member of the congregation and community. Not only was this church his first parish, he was this parish's first full-time pastor. During his time in the parish, the church grew from a very small core membership (of fifty or so members) to the vibrant middle sized congregation Linda found when she came there.[7]

To many in this congregation the previous pastor was a "family chaplain" (to use Arlin J. Rothauge's terminology), while to others who joined the church as it was experiencing its first period of growth, he was viewed as the "central pastor," and to those who joined the church as it grew even more, he was viewed as an "enabler and chief administrator." However, the previous pastor never assumed this last role in his own estimation. He was uncomfortable with delegation of responsibilities and the organization of the congregation into "program units." Instead, he continued to be led largely by the counsel of a small and highly vocal circle of persons who had been with the church from its beginning.

The church grew from its start-up as a "Family Church" with its chaplain to a "Pastoral Church" with its "central pastor." These transitions were met quite well by the pastor and those at the core of the church's leadership. Some of those who joined the church during its time as a "Pastoral Church" found themselves integrated to varying degrees of effectiveness into circles of some influence, though they never enjoyed the influence of those at the center of power. But while the congregation grew to the size of a "Program Church," the power of its leadership did not effectively shift in a corresponding manner. The pastor continued to try to lead by maintaining pastoral contact with the whole congregation, and those who had been with the church from its beginning as a "Family Church" and in its earlier years as a "Pastoral Church" tended to resist a shift toward more inclusive leadership. At the same time, there was a sense of discontent growing among the members of the church who had joined during the last five or six years, who wanted to share in the church's leadership, who wanted their ideas to be taken seriously, and who wanted to see the church expand its ministry programmatically. But when the pastor left, these changes had not occurred to a significant degree.

When Linda arrived, after an interim period of almost a year, she behaved toward the church as though it were a "Program Church," assuming that the members were accustomed to this sort of leadership. She observed that the governing board of the church was organized into a variety of committees, but she did not understand the significance of the fact that these committees were the work of the interim pastor and had only been in place on paper. She did not understand that they were not fully functioning.

She assumed that the congregation was prepared to work with her in a collegial fashion through a democratic organizational style of leadership. What she was not prepared for was the actual movement of power in the congregation.

She became aware of this when she made what seemed to her some minor changes in worship. The Monday morning after her second Sunday at the church, a member of the Pastor Selection Committee came to see her. He said that some people were very upset with some changes she had made in the worship service. One person, he said, had told him that he felt completely alienated from the church because of these changes.

Linda quickly went through the possible changes. She went to her filing cabinet and pulled out a copy of the worship bulletin and then pulled out a copy of one of her predecessor's bulletins. She came back to her desk and sat down.

"Let's see, Ralph, what changes have been made."

Ralph pulled his chair over to the desk to look at the bulletins.

"Well, we called the opening prayer a collect."

"Yeah, we never called it that before."

"Uh huh. And I moved the Apostle's Creed to a position after the reading of the lessons."

"Well, we have always had it at the end of the service. And we don't call the Scripture reading a lectionary. And the pastor has always read that. I think one thing the people are upset about is having a lay reader."

"But that is pretty much all the change we're talking about, isn't it."

"Well, I think the feeling is that you should have talked to the board before making any changes. And there are some people who could help you stay on track with this. We should have told you more so people wouldn't get upset."

"That raises a question for me, Ralph. Who is it that is upset? I mean, are there several people or is this just one or two, or what?"

"Well, it's not a lot of people. But they are people who are very involved in what the church does. And the concern is if you are making these changes, where will you stop."

"I'm willing to change these things back to the way they were before. I don't want to be perceived as changing lots of things right off the bat. But I've got to tell you I don't really consider these major changes. And I am a little concerned about how I am to know when I may be changing things that are perceived as major. You know what I mean?"

"The best thing to do is to talk to a few of the people who have been around here for a long time, to get a feel for that. They can tell you a lot better than I can. I haven't been here all that long."

Linda and Ralph's meeting ended pretty soon after this, but Linda was very concerned that she had hurt her leadership ability. She wanted these early months to go well. In the next few days, she discovered who it was who had objected to her changes, and she went to see her personally.

Mrs. Simpson was a matriarchal figure in the congregation. Her family helped found Grace Church. She was a large contributor to the church, and despite being nearly blind, she attended worship virtually every week. She was venerated by many in the church, especially among those who had been with the congregation from the beginning and those who had joined during its first period of growth some fifteen-to-ten years ago.

She had missed worship on Linda's first Sunday. When she sat down in her usual pew on that second Sunday and opened the bulletin to find that the order had changed, and then as worship started saw not only Linda process to the chancel but a lay reader as well, she said, just loudly enough for those sitting closest to her to hear, "I feel just like I have come to the wrong church."

And though her words were spoken softly and without any sort of bad intention, their effect was heard all over the parish that afternoon. Mrs. Simpson had been hurt because the new pastor was changing things.

Linda felt very bad about what had happened. "I should not have changed anything yet. I should have kept everything just like it was for at least six months, maybe even a year," she said to herself, "Now I am going to be known as someone who doesn't respect the way they have done things. People will look at me as someone who just changes things for the sake of change."

As soon as Linda discovered the source of the concern Ralph had raised to her, she went to see Mrs. Simpson for herself. They had tea together. They talked about Mrs. Simpson's life of leadership, spanning over half a century, in the church. Mrs. Simpson talked about the years when the congregation could only afford a pastor to come every other week. She talked about how the church had almost lost its property once, but how her husband Mr. Jack Simpson had saved the church's property. Mrs. Simpson, who had been reared in the Episcopal Church, distrusted what she saw as "high church" liturgy "intruding" into the Presbyterian Church. Linda listened mostly and talked very little. Before Linda left, however, Mrs. Simpson told Linda that there were some things she had been feeling needed changing. And Mrs. Simpson proceeded to provide her with a short list of two or three things that she wanted to see changed as soon as Linda could get to it.

Linda did not answer Mrs. Simpson directly—a fact that did not go unnoticed by Mrs. Simpson.

After the visit as she drove back to the church office, Linda turned this over in her mind. "I am in danger of getting a reputation for making changes, changes that have apparently threatened to alienate a trusted, venerated, and dearly loved member of this congregation. But just now in a visit with this very member of the congregation, I have been told that I need to make a few changes in the church's worship plans and education program. Is change the primary issue? Or is it just a presenting issue that is disguising the real issue?"

Linda mused for several days. After the furor died down, she received a phone call from another member of her Pastor Selection Committee, a successful businessman whose wife was in charge of the congregation's education program. On the phone he counselled her to be sure and check with some trusted people, people who had been in the congregation since its beginning, if she wanted to stay on track. "These are the people who are likely to stay here, you see." He then suggested those people who he felt would give her the best advice. "The point isn't so much change," he said,"but how you change, and who you have talked to."

It was then that Linda realized what had been missing in her analysis of the problem. He had told her what she had missed. "The primary issue," she reflected, "is not change, but control. My changes were *my* changes. I was perceived as being out of control and unpredictable. Maybe I should not have made a unilateral decision on the changes. But I'm not sure I would want to listen to the voices of only a very few. What I need to do is to start working within the whole structure that is available here, the committees of the governing board that are in place and the organizational officers. If I can help them become decision-making bodies, then changes can be made on the basis of our shared perceptions of need, and the changes could be more effective because there will be a built-in basis of support for them."

There are no bad guys and good guys in Linda's story. There are simply different people working with different perspectives on how to do what is right. And this is important.

Linda wants very much to be a good pastor and to serve her parish well. Ralph is concerned about the same things. So is Mrs. Simpson. So is the second member of the Pastor Selection Committee who called Linda. Each of them interprets the good of the parish as being tied up somehow with his or her own interests and with his or her own image of what the church is meant to be. Each one is influenced by specific dynamics that have emerged in the life of the church as it has grown from a small almost single-celled organism to a relatively large multicellular organism. Linda is discovering in this process that if she is to serve the congregation well, she must work with power and that she must understand the impulse to control, her own impulse and the impulses of others. And she is understanding that power and change must be intimately and intrinsically communal, recognizing at the same time the existence of power traditions that influence present attitudes as well as the newly emerging patterns of leadership that may be conflicting with the vestigial remains of the older traditions of power. Linda has recognized her initial misreading of the situation. She is beginning to understand that the change per se was only the irritant that precipitated her crisis. The fundamental issue, however, was not the specific change she made, but the perception that she was making changes without having sought the appropriate counsel.

Linda is convinced that change can be healthful to a congregation if it is the natural result of a congregation's growth and maturity, its continuing adaptation to meet new challenges and new awarenesses, or if it is as a matter of consensus, a response to a specific problem that needs to be solved. She also knows that change simply for the sake of change is not necessarily a sign of congregational health.

What Linda needs are some tools to help her analyze the total parish environment, her role as pastor, the best means to determine what changes need to be made, and how to make them. In the following sections, this is specifically what we shall attempt to provide for her.

When We Are Talking About Change, What Are We Talking About?

Change happens when something becomes different, when it is modified from what it was before. Thus change assumes that a thing is imperfect.

Change until very recently has not been considered a virtue, but a sign of defect. God in much classical theology was regarded as immutable, unchanging, and unmoving, *actus purus*. And so there has been built into the Christian church something of an unstated (but deeply felt) assumption that change is not generally for the good, and that at best it is an admission of our inability to correspond to the character of the immutable God whom we worship.

In the recent past, however, this rather static understanding of God has undergone some change of its own. People have become more comfortable with thinking of God (and, by extension, the church) in terms that allow a degree of change, movement, or process. Even those who continue to deny the possibility of mutability in the character of God (for some very good reasons) often will admit to the desirability of change in the church as the church attempts to come to terms with its environment in obedience to God.

Change, as we shall consider it, has two specific aspects: (1) change as problem-solving and (2) change as growth or adaptation.

Change as Problem Solving

While change as growth will be our primary concern, we feel that it may be helpful to discuss very briefly change as problem solving, if for no other reason than to differentiate between problem solving and change as growth.

The first thing that must be clearly understood is whether one is dealing with a problem or with a predicament. As Dr. Joe Gross, director of Pastoral Care at the Baylor Medical Center in Dallas, Texas, explains, problems "have solutions, predicaments don't." We have found this to be a helpful fundamental distinction. Many times pastors are called upon to "solve problems," especially in pastoral counseling situations. In fact, because of the nature of the situation, there is no "problem" whatsoever to be solved, only a "predicament." In the case of a problem, there are steps that can be taken toward a solution. But in the case of a predicament, the pastor may be able only to offer clarification of the situation and support to those involved.

Jay Haley, in one of the most helpful therapeutic guides on the market today, provides the essential starting point for change as problem solving. His comments are as applicable to church administration as they are to pastoral therapy. He says: "If therapy is to end properly, it must begin properly—by negotiating a solvable problem and discovering the social situation that makes the problem necessary. The act of therapy begins with the way the problem is examined. The act of intervening brings out problems and the relationship patterns that are to be changed."[8]

To deal effectively with a problem in the parish, having determined that we are dealing with a problem and not a predicament, we must negotiate the problem as something that can be solved and then examine the relational or systemic context of the problem. In other words, we want to ask, "How does this problem work?" and "For whom does it (does it not) work?"

Paul Watzlawick, John Weakland, and Richard Fisch, of the Mental Research Institute in Palo Alto, California, have described a four-step procedure for dealing with problems. Their procedure can be used to flesh out Haley's general therapeutic approach.

They tell us to:

1) Make a clear definition of the problem in concrete terms. The more concrete the definition the better.

2) Investigate the solutions that have been attempted so far. How have other people attempted to solve this problem? In what ways have these previous attempts succeeded (and failed)?

3) Clearly define the concrete change you want to achieve. On the basis of your analysis of the problem and your study of previous attempts to solve the problem, define how you will go about solving the problem in the most concrete terms you can.

4) Formulate and implement a plan to produce this specific change. When dealing with specific and concrete steps to solve a problem, one can easily evaluate the success or failure of a program of problem-solving. If a solution did not work, one can begin again, having the advantage of yet another attempt that can be listed under step number 2.[9]

It is absolutely essential to understand any change in relational or systemic terms, whether this change takes the form of problem solution, or growth and adaptation. And so before focusing on change as growth, we would do well to consider the role of the pastor as change agent within the congregational environment. What we have discovered about the pastor's role in that context applies equally whether we are considering the pastor as leader in the solution of problems or as leader toward organizational growth.

Control vs. Empowering:
The Role of the Pastor as Leader in the Parish

As we said in the beginning of this chapter, there are two kinds of power that can be exercised in any organization: the power that empowers others and the power that controls by limiting the power of others. In a paper written specifically for educational administrators, Thomas J. Sergiovanni notes this distinction when he contrasts those leaders who exercise the *"power to"* and those who exercise *"power over."* "Successful leaders," Sergiovanni continues, "know the difference."[10]

To borrow the terminology we found in Galbraith, the leader who exercises "power over" tends to rely too much on "condign power." This is the power that relies on "bully sticks" and "carrots," says Sergiovanni. Neither school administrators nor pastors have too many of these. And speaking specifically of pastors, neither do we find this form of leadership consistent with the idea of power expressed in the Christian faith, as we discussed earlier in this chapter. Flexible leadership requires the use of "condign" and "compensatory" power in specific kinds of cases where task-oriented maturity is low. But these kinds of power, especially "condign" power, can be easily abused. A flexible leader must know when to use it and when not to. But even more important, s/he must understand how to use it in an appropriate and sensitive manner and how to move beyond it, how to use even "condign" power in such a way that those who are being led are drawn toward higher levels of involvement in which they also become empowered. Even when a pastoral leader chooses to use "condign" power, it can and should be used in such a way so as not to disenfranchise those who are led. "Power over" is not an appropriate use of power even for the flexible leader because "power over" is designed to strip others of power.

"Instead," Sergiovanni explains, "successful leaders are more concerned with the concept of *power to*. They are concerned with how the power of leadership can help people become more successful, to accomplish the things that they think are important, to experience a greater sense of efficacy."[11]

Pastoral leadership follows this pattern when it is both successful and effective. It builds from the ground up, enlisting support through a sharing of a sense of mission and a common vision, to the building of a broad consensus and an empowering of many persons to carry out the shared goals, to the actual accomplishment of the goals in which the whole group can take pride. Such an approach is effective because it is based upon the involvement of others who invest themselves in the project. This is apparent. But this effectiveness is even more fundamentally possible because the entire approach recognizes the systemic and relational nature of power, which we have already observed.

We have been using both the terms successful and effective almost synonymously. However, we may understand our role as leaders better if we consider the way Hersey and Blanchard differentiate between the two in their study on "The Management of Change."

They write: "If an individual attempts to have some effect on the behavior of another, we call this stimulus attempted leadership. The response to the leadership attempt can be either successful or unsuccessful."[12] In the most basic analysis, the success of a leader is measured by whether or not those s/he attempts to affect do what s/he wants them to do.

For instance, let us suppose that Jerry, the pastor, wants the governing board of the church to purchase new choir robes. He decides unilaterally that he wants this done. He meets with the board and by the

force of his personality gets the funding. Then he picks out the robes.
He has the secretary order them. And the choir must now wear what he
has chosen.

On the face of it, Jerry has been "successful" as Hersey and Blanchard
are using the term. But if Jerry, along the way to achieving this goal, has
antagonized the choir director, the chairman of the worship committee,
eight members of the choir who love the old robes that were given in
honor of Mrs. Jones, a longtime member of the choir who died last year,
and the finance chairman, who wanted the money to be spent on something else, then Jerry has not been "effective." His desire to get this
specific goal accomplished was short-sighted folly. He can expect some
serious repercussions.

Let's suppose another scenario in another church. Marianne senses
that the congregation is in need of a new public address system for the
sanctuary. She has been asking some of the older persons if they can
hear her, and they cannot. So she goes to the chairman of the worship
committee and the chairman of the building and grounds committee to
bounce the idea of a new public address system off them. They ask her if
she can give them a few days to think about it and suggest that in the
meantime she might ask the choirmaster what she thinks of the idea.

In a week or so, after talking to the choirmaster and getting her
feedback, she returns to the two chairmen and discusses the idea with
them some more. The building and grounds chairman indicates that on
the face of it this is a good idea and suggests that he might talk to his
whole committee about it. He says that he will get back with Marianne
and the rest of the church board at the next business meeting.

As the idea is discussed, it is gradually owned by those who talk
about it, but as it is owned, it is altered. So by the time the idea has come
to the board meeting through the chairman of building and grounds, a
consensus of approval has already built in favor of the idea. But the idea
is no longer what Marianne had in mind in the beginning. She had imag-
ined a public address system that she had seen in a colleague's church.
This is not the system the board wants to vote on. But it is a system and
a good one, and Marianne is fairly well pleased.

What has happened is that *Marianne has been successful* in that
she has achieved the goal she wanted to achieve (the church will have a
good public address system installed in the sanctuary), and *she has been
effective* (the means by which she succeeded did not antagonize others

through controlling them, but empowered them to achieve the goal, allowing them to become participants in the shaping of the goal and in its achievement).

The merely successful leader achieved the goal but in a way that virtually guarantees limits to his success in the future. The successful and effective leader realized her goal but in a way that has greatly enhanced her power and that will contribute to her success and effectiveness in the future. The key to her effectiveness was her pursuit of participative or consensual change.[13]

Obviously the second model for (effective) leadership is generally preferable. But is it always? Hersey and Blanchard further contrast the two models in such a way that we can see that there are times when the first model for (successful) leadership is actually preferable, and there are many times when a combination of the two is even more preferable than either the first or the second alone. In order to understand why this is, let us reflect on the models more carefully.

Hersey and Blanchard explain that the first model (successful leadership) is based on "coerced change." The cycle of coerced change begins when the leader imposes change on the organization. The leader's decision directly changes the group's behavior and, in turn, the behavior of individuals in the group. Their attitudes are affected because they have been made to change. And finally, their knowledge will be affected as they are forced to come to terms (either positively or negatively) with the change. If they come to understand (on the knowledge level) the necessity for the change and come to appreciate it (on the level of their attitudes), then their individual behavior will be reinforced and as a group they may come to own the idea. This is especially true in the case of immature groups who are highly dependent on the direction of a leader and on fairly rigid structures of an organization.[14]

Hersey and Blanchard illustrate the cycle of coercive change as follows on page 61:

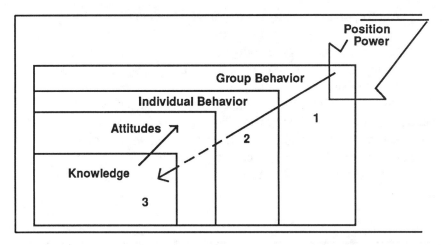

Figure 2: Coercive change cycle (Hersey and Blanchard)

Suppose a pastor moves into a rather isolated parish, one which has not been exposed to the uniform lectionary that follows the Christian calendar. The pastor might decide unilaterally that worship should be based on the lectionary. Using his position as liturgical leader, he makes the change. Then, carefully and methodically, he begins to explain the significance of the change in the hope that the members will come to appreciate the changed emphasis in worship. If the information is convincing and the attitudes of the parishioners are changed, they are enabled individually to "own" the change, and ultimately as a group can integrate it into their corporate life.

Coercive change begins its cycle from the top. By contrast, participative change is implemented at the level of the communication of new knowledge by a leader whose power is expressed more personally and collegially. When the new information is provided, the leader hopes that the individuals in the group "will develop a positive attitude and commitment in the direction of the desired change." The individuals begin to form new attitudes in reflection on the new information. They begin to formulate "goals and new methods for obtaining the goals." Then they will "attempt to translate this commitment into actual behavior." This, Hersey and Blanchard explain, is the most difficult stage in making changes through the participative model. It is one thing to be concerned about something, they say, it is quite another to actually get involved in doing something about it.

At this point in the process of participative change, they suggest the strategy of identifying informal (as well as formal) leaders in the group and concentrating on gaining the acceptance of these leaders for this change. Others in the group are more likely to agree to changes when they see that the changes meet with approval of persons they respect.[15]

When (and if) the group is able to move from new attitudes to changed behavior, the changes are likely to be both long lasting and generally accepted. This model works extremely well with more mature groups, however, the model is very slow in development.

Hersey and Blanchard illustrate the cycle of participative change as follows:

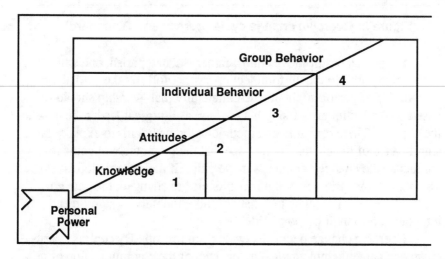

Figure 1: Participative change cycle (Hersey and Blanchard)

The advantage of the coercive model, as we might anticipate, is its speed and its utility with less "mature" groups. However, this model is highly unstable and frequently produces significant "animosity, hostility, and in some cases overt and covert behavior to undermine and over-throw."[16]

In terms of pastoral leadership, the model of participative change is more consistent with our understanding of power as empowering. There may be some specific situations, however, that call for strictly "executive decisions." And it is frequently the case that a pastor will be called upon to provide a strong sense of direction (toward what he or she believes are the most appropriate goals of the church) while allowing considerable room for the group to be positively led into a fuller understanding of why these are the appropriate goals. In these cases, the pastor actively and intentionally combines the two models so that there is a degree of decisiveness (in terms of directedness toward the larger goals) with a high degree of group participation (building a consensus on the basis of knowledge acquisition and changes in attitude). As we have noted before, effective leadership involves considerable skill and flexibility and depends upon the maturity level of the group in a specific circumstance.

Consensus and Change

Not long after arriving in his second full-time parish, Michael had an experience that helped him to understand the way change is served by the development of consensus.

It happened at my first session meeting. We were almost at the end of the agenda, when under "New Business: Misc." an elder said, "Well, you know, I don't have any real strong feelings on this myself, but there's been a lot of talk about what to do with the church's silver service. And I think we ought to settle this thing."

Now the church's silver service had been given to the church in loving memory of one of the oldest families in the church. These were great patriarchal and matriarchal figures, long since gone, but always present in spirit. The silver service was restricted for use at weddings in the church. For many years this had not been a problem. The church had not been terribly large, but, even more important, the church was practically all "family."

But the year before an accident happened that caused all sorts of ill feeling. A young woman who had joined the church, but whose family did not have historic ties to the church, had been married in the sanctuary. Her family had used the silver, and in the course of the reception, a leg had been broken on the tea pot. The family had agreed to pay for having the piece fixed, but there was a lot of concern about what to do with the service after it was fixed.

The elder who brought the question up said that there were some folks who felt the silver should be kept under lock and key and only used at official functions of the church and then only under the supervision of a few specific people.

Another elder made the rather heated suggestion that the silver might best be melted down into a silver calf so we could at least clarify what we were doing with it. This suggestion was met with a combination of chuckles and "harrumphs."

After we discussed the subject—all of which was news to me—for about twenty minutes, somebody made a motion (either to let everyone use the silver or not to let anyone use it—I forget exactly what it was), somebody else seconded it, and they voted. And they tied! Then they all looked to me.

Those who are familiar with Presbyterian church polity know that a pastor, as Moderator of the Session, votes only in case of a tie. They tied the vote and looked at me. And I looked at them. And they looked at me. And finally I said, "Okay, you want me to break this tie."

"Yes," someone said, "That's what you've got to do."

"And you will abide by whatever decision I make, despite what side you are on?"

There were some nods of agreement.

"Well, here is my decision. Next Sunday afternoon at five o'clock a committee of seven people, two from the session, two from the diaconate, two from the Presyterian Women, and I will meet here in my office for a period of one hour. We will, as a group, draw up a list of guidelines to determine the exact procedures that will govern the use of the church's silver services. If they can agree on the drawing up of these guidelines, we will have a set of procedures to guide us. If they cannot agree on the guidelines in an hour, then we will have no guidelines and anyone who wants to may use the silver.

The next Sunday afternoon at five o'clock the committee got together. We listed the reasons why the silver was important to us, what our concerns were regarding its use, and who was likely to want to use it in the future. Then we sat down to writing a set of guidelines to govern its use. Nobody got everything he wanted, but everyone did get something. We discovered that pretty nearly everyone shared the same concerns, values, and traditions, though we did have some conflicts regarding the utility of the pieces in question. But because of the shared concerns, values, and traditions, we had plenty of room to come to a consensus. And because it was a consensus, we could all live with the guidelines.

What I attempted to do, in this circumstance, was to develop a consensus. But I could only do this from a point of pastoral crisis, the moment when the decision fell into my lap as moderator of the session. I was completely directive in the sense that I refused to allow a decision to be arrived at by any means other than consensus. But I was nondirective in the sense that consensus ruled.

It all worked out very well. But what is really frightening to me is how close I came to deciding for or against the original motion.

Persistence and Change

We began this study by saying that this book is written *to help curates come to terms with their cure.* And one of the most difficult aspects of our cure is the maintenance of a balance, or perhaps better a tension, between the pastoral role as representative of the congregation's persistence and the role of change agent. The pastor represents a sense of continuity within the life of the congregation, not least because the pastor, as priest, stands as the representative of the Word of God among a particular people.[17] He or she also represents a visible and concrete tie to the theological and social traditions of a particular church, its sense of belonging to some larger movement within the universal church's history. Schism is abhorrent even to schismatics. Few churches have survived for long without some sense of continuity with the larger church's history. Some denominations (often unofficially, but popularly) have even manufactured imaginary histories that tie them somehow to the apostolic church.[18] The pastor serves as a living symbol of the church's sense of continuity to this tradition.

The pastor also represents more specifically the persistence of a particular congregation, its sense of "thereness" as some call it. The congregation has been concretely "there" as a believing body, holding certain things precious, holding other things to be spurious, through a personal and specific history; the pastor represents a continuation of this tradition. The Church persists. We can see that in the pastor's identification with its concrete history, its traditions, and its values. This church has chosen to be this way and not some other way, and the pastor it has chosen represents this fundamental choice.

But if a pastor is only the representative of the corporate persistence of these people, he or she cannot also serve as a catalyst to help the congregation to adapt, to grow, and to change because such a catalyst, of necessity, makes a friend of the uncomfortable, that which cannot be simply assimilated into the existing structures of persistence. The pastor, as change agent, leads the congregation into new possibilities, possibilities that are *new* often by virtue of the fact that they were previously considered impossible or perhaps undesirable or unlikely. The leadership role of the pastor not only includes his representation of the *status quo* but an element of risk taking, a willingness to make uncomfortable those who have grown comfortable.

A similar tension in leadership between the leader's role as representative of the group's persistence and the leader's role as change agent has been observed in educational administration. Robert G. Owens describes this tension in his study of "The Leadership of Educational Clans." The effective leader understands his or her role as "symbolic leadership," as he puts it. S/he "signals and demonstrates to others in the clan what is important, what is valued, what is wanted, what goals override others." But as symbolic leader s/he does not simply represent the status quo. The symbolic leader also "creates and communicates a vision for others in the clan, describing a desired state of affairs, one better than the present." In order to fulfill the role of symbolic leader, in order fully to represent the values and desires and goals of the group, s/he must have a firm grasp of the history, traditions, legends, past and present heroes, important rituals, and customs of this group and must be able to communicate his or her valuing of this common ground so that s/he can be counted on as the person (above all others) who will act to "preserve the traditions that already exist." And while doing this, the symbolic leader must have a clear sense of direction about the future directedness of the group so as to facilitate the building of "new higher-order traditions."[19]

We have described these two roles of the pastor as standing in a balance or a tension. If the pastor rests in either one or the other, he or she is likely to do considerable damage to the congregation and to him/herself. The pastor who represents the congregation's corporate persistence to the extent that s/he does not have the ability to stand over against this persistence likely contributes to a large degree of congregational stagnation. The pastor, however, who, in attempting to be a change agent, becomes merely an irritant to a congregation and does not identify fully enough with the traditions and values of a church, will be disregarded and eventually disowned.

For the pastor this tension can be troublesome and even painful. But it is a creative tension. And, in our experience, those who come to terms with it are consistently more helpful to their congregations than those who do not.[20]

Cognitive Styles and Effective Leadership: Another Parenthetical Remark

One of the most important advances in our understanding of effective leadership derives from research in the area of cognitive styles. This research has been carried out in response to questions raised by Carl Jung's study, *Psychological Types* (1921). Jung's ideas have received a great deal of attention in recent years, and so we will not spend too much time discussing them. But there are a few implications for leadership and change that we need to touch upon, if only very briefly.

Essentially, those who have studied this area in relation to management have followed Jung in determining that there are two sorts of perception. Those people who tend to lean more on their senses to provide for them a more literal or exact description of their environment, of things that happen around them, and things that may happen in the future are said to depend on *sensation*. Those people who tend more to rely on the subtle and often intangible connections between things, looking for the hidden meanings and possibilities in things that happen in their environment and things that may happen, are said to depend on *intuition*.

In addition to Jung's categorization of perception, he also determined two general categories of judgment, how people come to a critical assessment of things. Those people who tend more to make decisions on the basis of logic and rationality, those who pride themselves more on objectivity, are said to decide on the basis of *thinking*. Those who tend to make decisions more subjectively are said to judge on the basis of *feeling*.

Jung's analysis of perception and judgment is important to those who lead, chiefly, as Pat Burke Guild has said, for two reasons: (1) a leader should be self-aware in the development of his or her leadership abilities, and (2) the leader must work effectively with people who have different cognitive characteristics.[21]

For instance, the pastor who is highly intuitive in her perception and feeling oriented in her judgment will need to be aware of the cognitive needs of a board member who is perceptually sensate and oriented toward thinking in his judgment. It would be very easy for the highly intuitve-feeling oriented pastor to be viewed as a "fruitcake" by such a board member because the board member might not be able to see the "logical" connections that the pastor intuitively arrives at. And because the board member may not see the logic of an idea, he may not think it worthwhile. Such an intuitive pastor will have to work hard to flesh out ideas and to demonstrate logically their value in order to lead such a board member toward change. At the close of the book we have provided some exercises that should help pastors reflect on cognitive styles. We highly recommend that pastors work with these exercises, and if they have not already done so, take the Myers-Briggs Type Indicator to determine their own perceptual/judgment styles. This self-awareness will be most helpful in providing the pastor with insights into what must be done in dealing with the systemic (interpersonal) dynamics of the group in order to promote more participative change based on a broad consensus.

Change as Growth

When most of us think of change we think of change as growth, a congregation's adaptation to new developments or new goals. It is here, more than anyplace else, that our skills as leaders are called into question. To help us facilitate change as growth, we will do well to identify how changes occur in congregations and how we can facilitate positive changes.

First, we will consider the general pattern of organizational change. Then we will examine, in considerable detail and from a different perspective, the dynamics of group change and the elements of resistance to change that one should predict and indicate how we can deal sensitively and effectively with resistance.

Kurt Lewin, in what some have called the "pioneer work in change," identifies the pattern of what is generally referred to as "the process of change." The three phases through which an organization passes in the process of change are:

Unfreezing
Changing
Refreezing

Each phase in the process of change demands particular responses on the part of the pastor. And the demands made on the pastor are rather different from those made on a leader in other groups.[22]

Unfreezing. "The aim of unfreezing," write Hersey and Blanchard, "is to motivate and make the individual or group ready to change." As we have seen, the effective leader who encourages a high degree of participation in change begins by educating the individual or group, providing new information that will help to form new attitudes, thus paving the way for positive change. The pastor will want to include in this information a clear sense of how this change connects with the existing values and goals and traditional self-perception of the congregation, and how this change may call upon the congregation to develop new values and goals. The pastor will also want to provide information concerning the consequences for the congregation if they do proceed with the change or if they do not. Unfreezing involves a reinterpretation of the traditions, values, and goals of the congregation in order to ready the people to accept new possibilities. When unfreezing happens effectively, the group becomes motivated to make the change, that is, they come to own the change as a positive development and become committed to making it happen.

For example: The leadership of a downtown church in a large metropolitan area has determined that the congregation should provide some sort of ministry to street people, many of whom are in need of basic necessities for life. This is strongly felt and strongly expressed to the governing board of the church. After some study by the mission committee of the church and its staff resource person, it is decided that the congregation should provide a soup kitchen and clothes closet ministry to these people. The board, under the leadership of the pastor and professional staff, then proceeds to evaluate in what way this change can be understood in light of who this church perceives itself to be, what its mission is, what its values are, and where it sees itself as moving. The decision is made that these new ministries are appropriate not only in terms of the church's traditions, but in terms of new developments in its self-understanding. It is ready to make the changes necessary to provide this new ministry.

Changing. When unfreezing is effective, the congregation is prepared to change. Change itself occurs, according to Hersey and Blanchard, through either of two mechanisms (or through a combination of them): identification and/or internalization.

Identification is the process by which "one or more models [for change] are provided in the environment from which an individual can learn new behavior patterns by identifying with them and trying to become like them." **Internalization** is the process by which a person "is placed in a situation where new behaviors are demanded of him if he is to operate successfully in that situation."[23]

In the case of identification, the congregation is provided with a specific model for change and called upon to conform to it. In the case of internalization, a specific model for change is not provided, but the group is called upon to cope with its environment by providing itself with a new model. Very often change occurs in a congregation by a combination of identification and internalization. A broadly conceived model may be provided, for instance, while the details of the model may be developed as the congregation responds to the new demands of the total situation.

In the situation we have taken as our example, the downtown church has communicated with the congregation its concerns about a new ministry and has begun to put flesh on the skeleton of its idea. The leadership has, to an extent, provided a model that demands identification on the part of the congregation as a whole. And yet there is much in this model that remains to be decided by those in the congregation who have committed themselves to the task itself. They, as the group responsible for the continued effectiveness of the new ministry, will invent the model in terms of its actual operations and will invest it with its distinctive personality. To this degree, it will be a matter of internalizing the new model as the ministry is owned by the congregation as *their* ministry. The leadership will be wise to leave a high degree of this internalization to those in the congregation who will be most directly concerned in the maintenance and the promotion of the new ministry.

Refreezing. The change stage of the process is, however, somewhat unstable in and of itself. What is needed, therefore, is a process by which the newly-acquired change is integrated as a patterned behavior in the life of the congregation. This integration of the change model may have occured naturally if the people arrived at the new model through a process of internalization. But, especially if the model was provided for their identification, it will be necessary for the group to own the model as theirs by coming to the decision that this new model is essential to the life of the congregation as they now understand its traditions, values, and goals.[24]

For instance: The new ministry to street people will be owned by the whole congregation to the degree that they understand and commend themselves (as a whole) to be the church that serves in this way. When (or if) the congregation makes this step of integrating this new ministry into its understanding of who it is, the new ministry will become locked in as a persistent feature in the church's life.

Dealing Creatively with Resistance to Change

Obviously there are two points at which resistance would be most predictable in the process of change: (1) at the point of unfreezing and (2) at the point when the change is actually being made prior to refreezing. At both of these points, the individuals in the group are forced to question their self-understanding as a group. The pastor must be very sensitive to the group culture, to his/her dual role as representative of this culture, and as change agent at these two points in particular. Terrence Deal provides a method, similar in many respects to that employed by Roy Oswald's "historicizing design," that we can adapt for coping with these two moments of crisis in the change process.[25]

Deal attaches particular significance to the intrinsic power of a group to retain its existing culture (culture = "the way we do things around here"). Culture, whether in schools, in corporations, or in congregations, is "an all-encompassing tapestry of meaning" which is "transmitted from generation to generation."[26]

And the means by which this "tapestry of meaning" or culture is interpreted by members of the group is (as we have seen repeatedly) through its "shared values," "heroes," "rituals," "ceremonies," "stories," and "cultural network" (what Deal describes as "a collection of informal

priest/esses, gossips, spies, and storytellers whose primary role is to re-
inforce and to protect the existing ways").[27]

The degree of resistance a particular change meets often corresponds to how this change is perceived as threatening the existing culture
of a group. The congregation will want (instinctively) to interpret the
change in light of its culture (as this culture is transmitted and maintained
through its shared values, heroes, rituals, ceremonies, stories, and cultural network). Deal observes that the only way that resistance to change
can be overcome and lasting change can be effected is through the estab-
lishment of "transition rituals" that identify and reiterate the existing
culture of the group while providing the possibility for new meanings
and values. In other words, if new growths are to be nurtured, they must
be grafted securely onto old roots.

The development of "transition rituals" which harken back to the
symbolic touchstones and transmitters of the existing culture, its shared
values, heroes, rituals, ceremonies, stories, and cultural network, provides
a means to introduce changes while guaranteeing a sense of continuity
within the life of the congregation. Deal encourages leaders to use the
following kinds of strategies in order to overcome resistance of change.
We have adapted these strategies for congregational use.

The first three of these strategies could form a group activity at a
family night supper. Someone could make plans to videotape the discussion or to map the discussion on butcher paper for the whole group to
see.

— **Recreate the history of the congregation.** Assist the congregation in recounting its past, its defeats, and its successes. A church history
is never simply a recounting of facts, but is an expression of a congregation's self-perception. A pastor who does not know the "history" of his
or her congregation will have a very hard time serving as its representative.

— **Articulate shared values.** Help the members of the congregation express what it is they value and why they value it. These values
may not simply bubble to the surface on their own—as abstract ideas—
but may be more easily discerned in tandem with the recounting of the
church's history and the celebration of its heroes.

— **Anoint and celebrate heroes.** Every organization has a "pantheon of heroes." When a group is able to talk about them, they are able
to give "tangible human examples of shared values and beliefs."

— **Reinvigorate rituals and ceremonies.** "Rituals," Deal explains, "provide regular and special occasions for learning, celebrating, and binding individuals to traditions and values." As part of the recounting of the church's history, it may be possible to discern rituals and ceremonies that were once valued, but have been left behind for one reason or another. These may be recovered or may be reinvested with meaning by inclusion in new rituals and ceremonies.

—**Tell good stories.** Our stories identify who we are and who we want to be. It is possible for these stories, which may not be part of the church's history, to be brought into the church's life through sermons, newsletter articles, or teaching sessions, so that the congregation can evaluate its life in light of new narratives.

—**Work with the informal network of cultural players.** Recognize these people as bearers of the church's culture and involve them wherever possible in the changes to be made. Otherwise these people may feel estranged and may sabotage change.

Let's return to the large downtown church that is implementing a new ministry to feed and clothe street people to see how some of these strategies can be put into effect.

Those leaders who are responsible for starting up the new ministry are aware that this same church remembers with pride that it was the one church in their state who, under their beloved pastor Dr. Harold Campbell MacKinnon, fed those who were out of work during the dark days of national crisis in the Great Depression. They will, as they begin to rally support for the new ministry, demonstrate the church's continuous commitment to feeding those in need. In particular they will make contact within the cultural network of their congregation with those who, in days gone by, were instrumental in serving as helpers in "Dr. MacKinnon's Kitchen," as it was called. The start up of the new ministry will ritualize this continuity by asking these people to participate in the opening ceremonies and by speaking in favor of the venture in a mission update at the monthly fellowship suppers.

Another closely related reason that change is sometimes resisted has to do with the perception among some in an organization that the group is functioning better than it actually is. They are likely to respond to a proposed change with the attitude (if not the words) "don't fix what isn't broken." John Champlin has described this phenomenon as a form of "protective self-hypnosis." He explains: "We want to believe we are doing the right thing; in the absence of clear, objective feedback about our performance, we reassure ourselves about our high productivity."[29]

In the public school program that Champlin worked with to deal with this type of resistance to change, teachers were required to provide "a written philosophical premise that would establish a reason for all our instructional decision making." When they had to think through the things they had been doing on "automatic pilot," they soon eliminated (on their own) many of the things they did. The teachers were then given the "specific training" that they would need in order to work effectively in the new programs that were being devised.

What happened, in effect, was that the teachers themselves unfroze the system by critically evaluating the way things were done. They understood, in light of their own critical assessment of the system that changes had to be made. Then they were prepared to respond more positively to the changes introduced and were given the tactical support needed to accomplish them.

Probably the single most important thing for the pastor to come to terms with when s/he is acting as change agent and has met with resistance is that conflict is potentially creative, but that it must be dealt with in a way that encourages people to retain their self-esteem. In other words, the pastor needs to resist the temptation (and it is a temptation) to approach conflict as a competitive situation in which one person will win and the other will lose. The only situation in which a pastor ever "wins" is a situation in which the other "wins" as well. Any real victory is the victory of the relationship over competitiveness and excessive self-centeredness.[30] Which obviously means that the pastor who wants to lead a congregation in a way that is open to positive change must be willing to express him/herself assertively and negotiate honestly.

A Model for Understanding and Guiding Change as Growth in the Congregation

One of the most helpful models for understanding and encouraging positive and lasting change in an organization was developed by a team of educational management specialists and was reported in the journal of the Association for Supervision and Curriculum Development.[31] After painstaking research into schools *that change successfully*, this team reported several general characteristics of positive change upon which they developed their strategies.

They found:

1) *"Change is a process, not an event."* Change is not simply the handing over of a new program. It is a systemic process with a time line of its own, that frequently lasts over a period of years.[32]

2) *"Change is accomplished by individuals."* Change is not some nebulous, abstract, impersonal idea. Change affects specific individuals, and it is on individuals that our primary focus must be placed.[33]

3) *"Change is a highly personal experience."* Individuals are different. People do not simply behave collectively. While recognizing the systemic implications of change, room must be allowed to understand the uniqueness of individual responses to change. And "Change will be most successful when its support is geared to the diagnosed needs of the individual users... Paying attention to each individual's progress can enhance the improvement process."

4) *"Change involves developmental growth.* We have discovered from studies of change that the individuals involved appear to express or demonstrate growth in terms of their feelings and skills."

5) *"Change is best understood in operational terms."* People relate to change in terms of what it will mean to them or how it will affect them in the specific duties, responsibilities, and interests in the organization.[34]

6) *"The focus of facilitation should be on individuals, innovations, and the context."* Leaders often tend to understand a change in terms of a new program or a new curriculum they are introducing, or a new building they want to build. But in doing this, they tend to forget that these things alone do not make change. "Only people can make change by altering their behavior."[35]

Looking at a variety of schools, the team saw a pattern emerge whenever changes were introduced. Although their description of the pattern (which they called "the stages of concern") is directly related to the classroom, the pattern also emerges in pastoral ministry, as we shall see.

The Stages of Concern

Stage 1: Awareness
When a person first learns that a change is in the works, his or her first response is at the simple level of **awareness**. S/he might initially say something to the effect of: "I am not personally concerned with this innovation." In other words, s/he distances him/herself from the proposed change. But as it becomes clear that the change will affect him or her, the teacher begins to move on to the second stage of concern.

Stage Two: Informational
The next level assumes some amount of interest in the change. The person identifies it as something that will affect him or her. And so the person is likely to want more **information**. S/he may say, "I would like to know more about this."

Stage Three: Personal
The third level begins to make actual contact with the change on a **personal** level. The informational level was more casual, more general. Now a person wants to know: "How will using it affect me?"

Stage Four: Management
The next level of concern is the **management** level at which a person will ask operational questions such as : "I seem to be spending all my time getting material ready." They are integrating the implications of the change into their own activities, looking at how it will (or will not) work.

Stage Five: Consequential
And on the next level, the **consequence** level, a person is making application beyond him/herself to the longer-term consequences of the innovation. A classroom teacher might ask: "How is this change affecting my pupils?" A board member in a congregation might ask: "Is this program making a difference, either positively or negatively, in our community?"

Stage Six: Collaborative
At the next level of concern, a person may express a concern for **collaboration**. S/he might ask: "I am concerned about relating what I

am doing with what other people in my department are doing." Supposing the change has to do with new curriculum for a junior high class, the superintendent and teachers in that department might ask, "How will the use of this new curriculum affect the students' entry into the senior high class next year?"

Stage Seven: Refocusing

And at the final level of concern, referred to as the **refocusing** level, a person will naturally begin to respond to the change with modifications. The person has, to some degree, "owned" the change, but in "owning" it s/he may feel the need to alter it. At this level, a person is likely to say, "I have some ideas about how this could work even better."[36]

For those of us in pastoral ministry, these levels of concern are clearly identifiable. Frequently, when an idea is first introduced, we may meet with a response that is not unlike the first step of grief, that of denial. This corresponds to a reaction educational researchers observed in the initial stage of awareness. Someone may communicate (verbally or nonverbally): "I am not concerned about this innovation. t does not affect me."

The pastor then may choose to respond or "intervene" in a man-ner corresponding to the appropriate stage of concern. And at the level of awareness, the appropriate response is to involve people in discussions regarding the change that is being proposed or introduced.[37] This also fits with what we have learned about participative change. The pastoral leader, if s/he is to be an effective leader, must respect the process and let the process work, moving along with it naturally, responding appropriately rather than trying to force the process to move in a way that is not appropriate to its own "life."

Having discovered that there is a change in the works, *people will naturally want to know more.* And, as we have seen already, "the sharing of clear and accurate information" about the change is essential to the involvement of people in any innovation. There is no way to change attitudes about something until we have provided the necessary information.

As we have seen, the next level, the personal level, includes the feelings and attitudes that people will have in reaction to a change and to the information they have received about it. They ask how it will affect them personally. At this level in particular, those in leadership will need to listen to specific personal concerns so that people can understand that they are being heard and will be heard as individuals. The leaders will want to maintain their commitment to the innovation while resisting any temptation to push it off on others.

Those in leadership will need to listen in a different way at the level of management concerns. At this level people are likely to bring very specific operational questions to leaders. For instance, supposing that the church building is to be used by a group of people who have never before used the facilities, someone on the buildings and grounds committee is likely to want to know, on the personal level, if he is responsible for turning off the lights when they leave. But on the management level he may want to know, more generally, if he isn't responsible for the supervision of the building when it is in use, who is?

The leaders will want to deal specifically with "nuts-and-bolts" operational questions, providing clear steps and procedures, focusing on the "how-to" side of things, answering logistical questions, and predicting the demands the change is likely to make on the congregation in the immediate future.

This leads us to consider the concerns of the congregation as to the impact this change will have on its future. When these questions come up, it may be wise for the leaders to suggest that a group of concerned people visit another church that has been doing the same thing for a long time so that they can see what sorts of problems might arise in the future and how they might deal with them.

When the change is well underway, those involved in it will want to understand how they can work better together. The leader can serve best by providing opportunities for those who want to collaborate to do so, but, s/he should not attempt to force collaboration on everyone.

And eventually if the changes are effectively accepted by the congregation as their own, the point will be reached when some persons will assess the program in terms of how well it is working and will have ideas for its improvement. These people need to be heard and encouraged. They need to have their ideas and energies channeled in ways that are productive rather than counterproductive. The pastor and other leaders should "be aware of and willing to accept the fact that these people may replace or significantly modify existing innovations."[38] But if the pastor and leaders are going to lead with the kind of power that empowers, indeed that multiplies the effectiveness of the congregation, they must be willing to let go of control over new programs so that the congregation can integrate the changes into its cultural life.

The pastor, in particular, will have to be aware that individuals reach different stages of concern at different times. S/he must be flexible enough to deal with individuals at their own levels of concern. And when differences arise (as they inevitably will), the pastor needs to be able to respond to parishioners in ways that create "win-win" rather than "win-lose" scenarios. This requires a maturity of pastoral leadership in which parishioners are encouraged by their pastor to express themselves, even to disagree about changes that are proposed, in an environment in which they will feel accepted and affirmed.

Again we observe that the pastor's leadership, if it is to be effective and successful leadership, must be characterized by flexibility. And while flexible in leadership, the pastor must remain true to a personal and pastoral center that corresponds to his or her perception of personal and spiritual authenticity. Achieving and maintaining this balance of flexibility and consistency is a great challenge for the pastor. But this is a tightrope worth learning to walk.

The Curate as an Interpreter of Congregational Life

In John Bunyan's classic allegory, *The Pilgrim's Progress*, Christian at a critical moment in his journey visits "the House of the Interpreter." The Interpreter leads Christian from room to room, showing him through vivid images the condition of his spiritual life and the consequences that lie in store if he should choose specific paths. Bunyan makes it clear that Christian is free to hear and to accept or to reject the reflections of the Interpreter, and after their interview, Christian is given insight and courage to meet the often awesome challenges of the road.

The pastoral leader, as one who has in his or her charge "the cure of souls," is also an interpreter, an interpreter of the life of a congregation. At critical moments in the life of a parish, the interpreter leads the congregation to reflect on who it is, what it has accomplished in the past, what it is about now, how it defines itself as a church, where it wants to go in the future, and how it can get there best. S/he assists the congregation in understanding the consequences that are in store should they choose one path while leaving other paths unchosen. And in all of this ministry of interpreting, the congregation finds itself free to respond. Indeed the interpreting, if it is done well, should enable the congregation to sense greater, not lesser, freedom as it is guided in its exploration of the possibilities and consequences that lie ahead.

The pastor who seeks merely to manipulate a congregation will in the course of manipulation also attempt to limit congregational power. "The cure of souls" will be distorted into a kind of tyranny in which persons will be denied their freedom and the congregation will be limited to express its corporate life only inasmuch as it conforms to the image of the pastor.

By contrast we have noted the way in which successful and effective pastors contribute to the empowering of a parish, how they build creative consensus, maintain the balance between their representation of the congregation's continuity and the need for change, how they adapt readily to various cognitive styles and models of leadership and remain responsive to the needs of individuals as the parishioners pass through the various stages of change. In all of this, the central issue at stake has been something at once more important and yet more elusive than simply leadership style or managerial competence; it has been our participation as pastors in Christ's "cure of souls." This is the center around which all else moves as we attempt to interpret the life of the congregations placed in our "charge." And it is this Curacy of Christ that finally evaluates our success or failure as pastors.

Concluding Summary: A Portrait of the Curate

What we have attempted to provide in this study of power and change in parish ministry are a variety of perspectives for reflection on what is happening in real life pastoral situations. Many issues have emerged, some we had anticipated when we began, others we had not. We hope that this study has proven helpful in identifying ways in which we may perform our ministry as pastoral leaders so as to empower the people of the church to explore and to employ their gifts for the good of the whole Body of Christ.

Before directing your attention to the section of reflective instruments, let's take just a moment to summarize what we have found. And as we do, we may observe something like a portrait of the effective and successful curate emerging from this study.

The curate, we have observed, is one whose pastoral ministry is characterized by a dual role. His or her "cure" is a *"healing cure,"* a *shepherding* and *caretaking cure* in which parishioners are assisted toward health and wholeness, but this "healing cure" is exercised in the context of a *"ruling* cure." The curate is a person who *heals* through his or her *leadership* even while s/he *leads* through his or her *"caring."*

Pastoral leadership is not simply a given, however. Its effectiveness and its success depend on whether or not a pastor is perceived by a congregation as authentically caring and authentically competent. The pastor who is perceived as authentic by his or her parish is invested with a significant share of authority (which pertains specifically to the pastoral role) and personal power (which accrues to the pastor over a period of time as his or her leadership is proven in concrete situations in the life of the congregation). But having said this much, as important as it is, we have not yet penetrated to the heart of pastoral authority and power.

The heart of pastoral ministry, we have said, is personal, spiritual, and *essentially theological.* Our pastoral ministry, as a comprehensive cure of souls, is grounded in our participation in Christ's Curacy over all souls. The pastor, therefore, needs to understand the dynamics of power and change in human organizations, and s/he must be able to interpret the meaning of power and change in social, cultural, psychological, *and* theological terms. We have observed how this can be done.

The goal of this analysis has been to provide an interpretive framework within which pastors can exercise their "cure," especially when this "cure" involves change. To this end, we have paid particular attention to the stages and the characteristics of change and to the role of the pastor as a representative of congregational continuity and as a change agent. We have paid particular attention to our responsibility to empower congregations to change. Our concern in this is to avoid the very real temptation to inflict upon a congregation a narrow image of its future based on our individual perception. Instead, as pastoral leaders, we enter into a dialogue with congregations to help them to change in ways appropriate to their perception of who they are and their vision of their purpose. We understand this empowering role as more appropriate to our pastoral ministry and provide several models that may help in interpreting the life of a congregation for the purpose of encouraging change.

As we have said from the beginning of this study, this book is a "curate's" tool, a practical device to assist pastors in their cure of souls.

"curate's" tool, a practical device to assist pastors in their cure of souls. In the following section we have provided several instruments to provide further assistance in reflecting on pastoral ministry. These instruments are laid out roughly following the development of the text of this book so that one may relate them directly to what has been read in the preceding chapters.

NOTES

1. The Acts of the Apostles 1:8.
2. Lord Acton's words appear, incidentally, in a letter to Bishop Mandell Creighton, April 3rd, 1887.
3. Gregory Bateson, *Steps to an Ecology of Mind* (Northvale, NJ: Jacob Aronson, Inc., 1972/1987), 494. Bateson's remarks appeared originally in a paper he gave, entitled "Pathologies of Epistemology," at the Second Conference on Mental Health in Asia and the Pacific, 1969, at the East-West Center, Hawaii.
4. Elias Canetti, *Crowds and Power* (New York: Continuum, English translation, 1962), 204ff.
5. C.S. Lewis, *The Screwtape Letters* (New York: Macmillan, 21st printing, 1974), 37-38.
6. Louis Adams, to whom we have already referred, suggests the following resources as being especially helpful in this context: Michael Foucault, *Power/ Knowledge: Selected Interviews and Other Writings* (New York: Pantheon Books, 1980), and H. Dreyfus and P. Rabinow, Editors, *Michael Foucault: Beyond Structuralism and Hermeneutics* (Chicago: University of Chicago Press, 1982).
7. Arlin J. Rothauge provides a very helpful analysis of the significance of size to the nature of a Church's ministry. In Rothauge's terms, this parish had grown from a "Family Church" of 50 members to a "Program Church" of 150-350 members, passing through (and spending the majority of its parish life as) a "Pastoral Church" of 50-150 members. See: A. J. Rothauge, *Sizing Up a Congregation* (New York: The Episcopal Church Center, 815 Second Avenue, NY 10017). We are deeply indebted to Dr. Rothauge for our own analysis of this situation, from the perspective of church size and ministerial role.
8. Jay Haley, *Problem Solving Therapy* (New York: Harper Colophon Books, 1976), 9.
9. Paul Watzlawick, John H. Weakland, Richard Fisch, foreword by Milton H. Erickson, *Change: Principles of Problem Formation and Problem Resolution* (New York: W.W. Norton & Company, 1974), 110-115. Reprinted by permission of W.W. Norton and Company, Inc. Copyright 1974 by W.W. Norton and Company, Inc.
10. Thomas J. Sergiovanni, "The Theoretical Basis for Cultural Leadership," in *Leadership: Examining the Elusive*, 1987 Yearbook of the Association for Supervision and Curriculum Development, Linda T. Sheive and Marian B. Schoenheit, editors (ASCD, 1987), 122. Reprinted with permission of the Association for Supervision and

Curriculum Development. Copyright 1987 by the Association for Supervision and Curriculum Development. All rights reserved.

11. Ibid., 122.

12. Paul Hersey and Kenneth H. Blanchard, "The Management of Change," in *Organizational Behavior and Management: A Contingency Approach*, Henry L. Tosi and W. Clay Hamner, editors (Chicago: St. Clair Press, revised edition, 1978), 506ff.

13. Ibid., 506-509.

14. Ibid., 511.

15. Ibid., 510.

16. Ibid., 512.

17. Bruce Reed provides a helpful discussion of the concept of representation in terms of the priest as representative of God to a congregation, and as representative of the people to God. His thought here parallels our own concerning our finding our vocation as curates in the Curacy of Christ. See Bruce D. Reed, *The Dynamics of Religion: Process and Movement in Christian Churches* (London: Darton, Longman and Todd, 1978), 165-167.

18. We have in mind, in particular, the Southern Baptist mythology of the "Trail of Blood," a highly romantic pseudo-history that supposedly traced the origin of the Baptists through the history of the Church all the way back to John the Baptist. This mythology was popular in previous generations, most notably in rural churches, even though it was consistently debunked by Baptist academic historians. The myth illustrates not only the power of popular mythology, but the need for it in order to establish—in some form or the other—a sense of "apostolic succession."

19. Robert G. Owens, "The Leadership of Educational Clans," *Leadership*, Shieve and Schoenheit, 24-25.

20. A good tool to use in coming to terms with a congregation's corporate persistence, and a tool that would also be very helpful in attempting to understand how and where best to initiate change, is Roy Oswald's "historicizing design." This instrument was published by The Alban Institute in R. Oswald's "Planning with Norms, Myths, and Meaning Statements," *Action Information*, Vol. XIV, No. 5 (September/October 1988): 7-9.

21. Pat Burke Guild, "How Leaders' Minds Work," *Leadership*, Shieve and Schoenheit, 85.

22. Hersey and Blanchard, "The Management of Change," *Organizational Change and Development*, Tosi and Hamner, 522ff.

23. Ibid., 523.

24. Ibid., 523-524.

25. Terrence E. Deal, "The Culture of Schools," *Leadership*, Sheive and Schoenheit, 3-15.

26. Ibid., 5.

27. Ibid., 6.

28. Ibid., 13-14.

29. John Champlin, "Leadership: A Change Agent's View," *Leadership*, Sheive and Schoenheit, 56.

30. Robert L. Woolfolk and Franck C. Richardson, *Stress, Sanity and Survival*, foreword, Arnold A. Lazarus (London: Futura, 1979), 161.

31. Shirley M. Hord, William L. Rutherford, Leslie Huling-Austin, and Gene E. Hall, *Taking Charge of Change* (ASCD, 1987). Copyright 1987 by the Association for Supervision and Curriculum Development. All rights reserved.

32. Ibid., 5.

33. Ibid., 6.

34. Ibid., 6.

35. Ibid., 6-7.

36. Ibid., 31.

37. Ibid., 44.

38. Ibid., 45-46.

Reflection Instruments

Many of these instruments, though they were designed primarily for individual use, might also be used in clergy support groups. In this case, after taking a few moments to write answers to the questions, each pastor could read aloud his or her answers, asking for other members of the group to respond.

I have also recently found this sort of process to work well in conversation with a ministerial colleague who agreed to respond to specific concerns. His very responses helped me to uncover concerns I had not seen until that moment, although I thought I had reflected very carefully. Those who have read our previous article in Alban's *Action Information* on collegial supervision[1] may want to use that model in conjunction with these exercises.

1. List the first ten parishioners that come to your mind. Beside each name write how you think they perceive your spiritual or personal authenticity. Reflect upon your actions and attitudes that communicate these perceptions. Ask yourself: Are they appropriate? Am I revealing my true spiritual and personal authenticity? Are my personal and spiritual values of such a nature that they correspond to what these persons perceive as authentic? What actions or attitudes might need negotiation or even change?

1) _____

2) _____

3) _____

4) _____

5) _____

6) _____

7) _____

8) _____

9) _____

10) _____

2. List the names of parishioners you feel you have difficulties with. Regarding spiritual and personal authenticity, are you out of step with them? Ask yourself why this may be. Identify three possible ways you could begin to build bridges to "connect" with these persons. For instance: I might ask myself, "Why am I having a difficult time connecting positively with Ben Crawford? Is it because I am really so different from what Ben sees as an authentic pastor? Or, is it a problem of communication? Is there a 'meeting place' between Ben and me?"

Name: _____

Why are we out of step?

_____

_____

_____

How can I build bridges between us?

(a) _____

_____

(b) _____

_____

(c) _____

_____

(Repeat process for each name on your list.)

3. Identify fifteen to twenty people within the church who you feel are exceptionally able. Think of a project you are about to begin in the church. Check the names of people on your list that you feel would bring special talents to the project. Think about strengths and interests of each. *Write down* specifically how you would go about asking each to participate. Ask yourself: Do I approach them all in the same manner? Or, are there different ways in which I need to approach them? It is easy to think about people as possessing different gifts. But is it not possible that their uniqueness also requires varying styles of leadership? Reflect intentionally on this uniqueness and the special challenge it may pose for pastoral leadership in your own parish environment.

PROJECT: _____

Name of potential participant in this project:

_____

Strengths

_____

_____

_____

Interests

_____

_____

_____

How I will go about asking for his/her involvement in this project:

_____

_____

_____

(Repeat process for other names on your list.)

4. List three to five projects (thought up by others) that you have rejected for "good reason," but which actually were more plausible than you gave credit. In each case, ask yourself why you actually dismissed the project. A good question to ask is "What was I afraid of?" List your concerns, fears, anxieties, then ask yourself the second, and in many ways more important question, "Was my fear justified?"

1) _____

2) _____

3) _____

4) _____

5) _____

5. List three to five occasions in the past twelve months where you took credit for a success when it ought to have been shared by others. Resolve to stop this behavior.

1) _____

2) _____

3) _____

4) _____

5) _____

6. Identify ten specific values you have in common with your congregation as a whole. Place a check beside each value that you might emphasize to strengthen your bonds with the church.

Next list five values (if that is possible) that you do not share. Check those differences of values that might cause major conflicts.

Common Ground

1) _____

2) _____

3) _____

4) _____

5) _____

6) _____

7) _____

8) _____

9) _____

10) _____

Differing Values

1) ————————————————————————————————

2) ————————————————————————————————

3) ————————————————————————————————

4) ————————————————————————————————

5) ————————————————————————————————

7. List any complaints you receive about your style of ministry.
Reflect: Could these complaints result from a difference in value systems? Is it possible to negotiate and develop a style acceptable by both?
What behaviors, expectations, priorities may change? Are you willing to
make these changes?

Complaint:

_____

_____

_____

Could this be the result of different value systems?   _____

Is it possible to negotiate?   _____

What behaviors, expectations, priorities might change as a result of
this negotiation?

_____

_____

_____

_____

Am I willing to make these changes?   _____

(Repeat process for other complaints.)

8.   List the names of five colleagues whom you consider to be especially
>   — authentic
>   — successful and effective

Names of colleagues you view as especially *authentic*:

1) _____

2) _____

3) _____

4) _____

5) _____

Reflect: What is it that strikes me as authentic about them? Personal real-ness? Spirituality? Openness? Lack of Defenseness? ???

Names of colleagues you consider both *effective and successful*:

1) _____

2) _____

3) _____

4) _____

5) _____

Reflect: Why do I see them as effective and successful? Do they "get things done?" Is it that they are well liked? Do they maintain balance in their vocation? What is it that is particularly striking about their effectiveness and success as pastors?

9. Think back over your work experience for the past ten years.

A) Title one sheet of paper *"Competencies."*

List as many specific competencies that you demonstrate in leadership situations as you can. Include them all; none are too small or insignificant.

B) On the back of this sheet list areas in which you feel *"Less competent."*

Choose one area you perceive to be the most important to work on and devise a plan to improve this area.

Include in your plan:
– relevant reading material
– a support group
– a colleague or consultant who excels in this area
– a list of specific behavior and attitude changes
– a date for reviewing your progress in achieving behavior change.

10. Professional and interpersonal competence spring from competence of the Spirit.

Reflect upon how you daily nurture and develop your spiritual competence.

Are you doing anything intentional about your spiritual formation?

If not, where could you go to get assistance? (Denominational staffworkers? Your Bishop or Executive Presbyter or, if your denomination has one, a "pastor to pastors"? Trusted colleague? A seminary professor? A retreat center?)

Formulate a plan to begin your own spiritual discipline.

11. Examine your present activities and responsibilities in various segments of the community and the church-at-large. Your "extended power" may be greater than you are aware of.

In what ways do your activities in the larger community contribute to your power to get things done?

How does this seem to relate to your pastoral authority?

---

12. Using Blanchard and Hersey's classification of power, identify your own power base in dealing with the church's governing body.

Identify a church committee that is having difficulty functioning effectively.

Analyze the "maturity level" of each individual, and the group as a whole.

Examine specific breakdowns in task completion.

Identify the power base that would be the most effective leadership style with this group.

Follow the same procedure with a committee that is performing effectively.

13. Examine your most significant relationships within the parish.

Do you seek to
     1) *control* and have power over?
     2) or *empower* and facilitate power to?

If your answer is the former, *determine a plan to change.*

Begin with a committee or group that is moderately mature and effective and include in your plan:
    – a list of each member and their specific strengths (self-starter, dependable, task-oriented, etc.)
    – resources that you use and that would benefit the group.
    – what else ???

---

14. Acknowledging that most church members really do want to "do the right thing," identify members who differ significantly with your own method of problem solving, decision making, or _____. Reflect upon a recent conflict you may have had with one of them.

---

15. *Identify* those parishioners who may have usurped "headship" thereby *using* others in the community.

Develop a plan for helping them utilize gifts and contribute to the fellowship in a more appropriate way.

Consider:
    – who they are and how they handle other sorts of situations
    – what they are trying to accomplish (assuming that people's motives are generally altruistic in their own eyes)
    – ways to redirect (education, sermons, personal conversation, peer pressure, etc.)

16. Think about the most critical conflicts you now face in your parish.
Which are *problems* (which seem to have solutions)?
Which are *predicaments* (which seem to have no solutions)?

PROBLEMS   PREDICAMENTS

_____   _____
_____   _____
_____   _____
_____   _____
_____   _____
_____   _____
_____   _____
_____   _____
_____   _____
_____   _____

This exercise alone can be very beneficial for us as pastors, distinguish-
ing between those things we can change and those things we must simply
live with. To get a handle on this, go back to the section in chapter three
headed "Change as Problem Solving." Reread it with your own pastoral
situation in mind. Now ask yourself about each concern you have listed
in the problem column: Can I make a clear definition of this 'problem'
in concrete terms? If not, it may not be a problem at all. Continue on:
Can I investigate solutions that have been tried? Can I clearly define
concrete changes I want to see achieved? Can I formulate and implement a plan to produce these changes? If the "problem" can be dealt
with in these terms, it is a problem and can be solved. If the concern
does not respond to this sort of procedure, it is a predicament. Our pastoral strategy will depend on this determination.

17. Look back at the problems you have listed. Choose one problem you would particularly like to see resolved.

Analyze how the problem works.

Identify for whom does it work? for whom does it not work?

Now, following our procedure for solving problems, *determine a specific strategy to solve this problem.*

18. Think back over your ministry for the past few years.

Identify a conflict in which
    A) you succeeded (you got what you wanted) and were effective as
        well (people were with you in the decision).
    B) you were successful but ineffective.

Consider what you could have done differently to encourage those
parishioners to want to achieve the goal.

This may be an occasion to draw together a group of trusted parishioners
to help you evaluate your pastoral leadership in a specific project. In this
case, you may want to limit your own role in the group to laying down
the ground rules.
    – Ask the group (a small group of 5 or 6) to reflect on your leader-
ship in a specific project.
    – Ask a member of the group to moderate the discussion while you
take the role of observer, writing down their observations, but not
intervening to defend yourself or argue.
    – After you have explained clearly the meaning of successful and
effective for the purposes of this discussion, the discussion leader will
ask each member of the reflection group to answer these two questions:
    1) How was the pastor successful and effective in this project?
    2) How could s/he have been more successful and effective?
    – The pastor can record the responses, answer specific questions for
clarification, and thank the group at the end of the exercise.

*This group model is an adaptation of Bill Gould's very helpful model for
pastoral evaluation (understanding pastoral evaluation as the pastor's
own tool). He suggests that the pastor set up a group that rotates new
members into the group and old members out of the group periodically.
Group members answer individually these two questions from the pastor:
"What is it I am doing that is most helpful to you personally?" and
"What is it I am doing that is least helpful?" The pastor merely records
responses and thanks the group at the end of the exercise. We have
found this to be an enormously helpful—and simple—model for the
pastor's evaluation of his or her own ministry. (Bill Gould is director of
the Southwest Career Development Center, Arlington, Texas.)*

19.   Reflect on your strengths as a leader.

Identify times you were particularly good in terms of leadership flexibility, times when you responded well to different persons at their own levels of maturity and in ways appropriate to their own cognitive styles.

1) _____

2) _____

3) _____

4) _____

5) _____

Identify times you have chosen the appropriate power base in dealing with a situation.

1) _____

2) _____

3) _____

4) _____

5) _____

Identify *specific* things you do within or without the parish which extend your power beyond the "role" power.

1) _____

2) _____

3) _____

4) _____

5) _____

20. Hersey and Blanchard discuss the immature worker as needing more direction, while the mature worker is able to participate more fully at all levels of the task. Use the following reflection instrument to evaluate for yourself the maturity of the workers and how you must set your leadership strategy appropriately.

List two or three small projects that need to be done in the parish.

Look at the committees responsible for implementing the projects.

Before beginning each project analyze the maturity level of individuals in each group and each group as a whole. Determine appropriate leadership style you will need to assume. Identify informal leaders within the group who might be helpful in task completion.

Develop a concrete plan intentionally based on your analysis, using the map on the following page as a guide in analysis and planning.

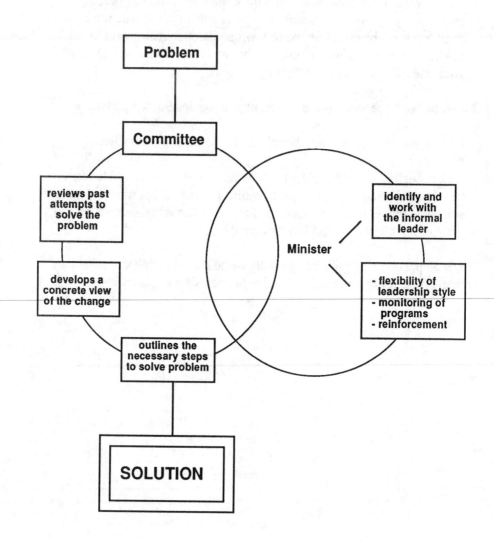

21. Take time to think about the people you admire and consider effective.

Write down their names.

Consider their successes and effectiveness.
     — What obstacles did they have to overcome?
     — What different people, pasts, traditions were they faced with?
     — How did they overcome?
     — What personal reserves/resources did they draw upon?

Determine some specific ways to model appropriately these behaviors.

---

22. For future reference when setting committees:

Identify fifteen people you perceive as mature, positive workers. (They want to move ahead and are capable of completing tasks). Keep these people in mind for future committee work.

Identify present "power" people in the church. Is their power personal, property, role, or a combination?

Identify people who create negative atmosphere or impair the work of committees (may be only in combination with certain others).

Identify combinations that are particularly effective.

23. Identify areas where you are backing the *status quo* in your parish.

How do you think the congregation perceives you in relation to your role as representative of the congregation's persistence or continuity with tradition? In what ways can you expand or deepen this role?

Identify areas where you act as a change agent. Examine these and determine the appropriateness of your actions. Would your leadership in change have greater effect in another area?

---

24. Jung's Cognitive Styles

A) Determine your own psychological type

  sensing<————————————————————————>intuitive

(We strongly suggest using the Myers-Briggs Type Indicator.)

B) Determine the psychological type of the members of:
   − the governing board
   − significant others in the decision-making body
  You can get a ball-park idea of this by asking such questions as:
Are they literal? Do they want exact descriptions? Do they want dates?
If so, they are most likely working from the sensing mode.
   Do they look for connections? Possibilities? Do their decisions look illogical? These will be intuitive workers.
   Looking at this list, place a check by the names of anyone you generally differ with in conflict. Compare their psychological type with your own.

Another exercise that comes highly recommended by Celia Hahn is to actually go through the Myers Briggs Inventory with the governing board. This is an exciting possibility that lets the entire board in on the way each person sees things, thinks, feels, and makes decisions.

25. In implementing change, map out the process and stages of change to keep in touch with what may be happening. (Map of change process appears below.)

Refer to the section in Chapter Three, titled "Change as Growth." Reread with your specific change in mind.

What is it that is going to be changed? How will that change happen? Who will it affect?

What shape will the unfreezing take? How will you help those involved become "ready for change"?

In the actual change, is the process one of identification or internalization?

By way of refreezing, how will you help the group "own" this change, incorporating it into the group's traditions as something consistent with their values and goals?

Consider use of Oswald's "historicizing design" in this context.

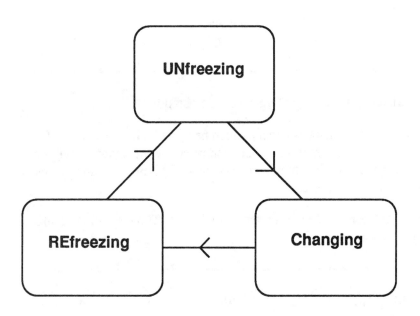

26. Identify five parishioners you perceive to be powerful.

1) _____

2) _____

3) _____

4) _____

5) _____

Using Galbraith's instruments of power (condign, compensatory, conditioned), label the power type of each person you list.

Next, determine the source of power (personal, property, and organization) for each. Remember that the source may be a combination of the three.

Understanding the source of power and how it is exercised will enable you to work with these people more effectively.

---

27. Planning for change: Organize a Celebration

Anytime major changes occur, human beings experience a crisis of identity. It is helpful to remember and celebrate the culture (traditions, stories, rituals) of the church and to prepare for new ideas and values to become a part of these.

Examine Terrence Deal's strategies in Chapter Three to help organize this celebration.

---

28. Identify areas in the church's life where the congregation is under "protective self-hypnosis."

Determine how to "break the spell" by specific reality testing.

29. Identify an area of change in the church that involves several people.

List the names of all involved.

Examine the reactions of each to the specific change.

Identify the stage of concern (Chapter 3) each person is operating from.

Next to each name, write the stage of concern and a brief plan that will be appropriate in guiding them to the next level.

---

30. Consider your present pastoral responsibilities.

What "sacred cows" did you inherit from your predecessor? A good way to determine this is to listen for: We *always*........ or We *only* ....

Determine which of these can be left alone for now and which need to be dealt with.

Working with willing members, plan to develop *new initiatives* while embracing the *old traditions*.

NOTE

1. Deborah and Michael Jinkins, "Increasing Competence in Ministry with Collegial Supervision," *Action Information*, Nov.-Dec. 1986.